HORIZON

JANUARY, 1963 · VOLUME V, NUMBER 3

HORIZON

A Magazine of the Arts

JANUARY, 1963 · VOLUME V, NUMBER 3

PUBLISHER
James Parton

EDITORIAL DIRECTOR
Joseph J. Thorndike, Jr.

EDITOR
William Harlan Hale
MANAGING EDITOR
Eric Larrabee
ASSOCIATE EDITOR
Ralph Backlund
ASSISTANT EDITORS
Ada Pesin
Jane Wilson
Albert Bermel
CONTRIBUTING EDITOR
Margery Darrell
EDITORIAL ASSISTANTS
Shirley Abbott, Caroline Backlund
Wendy Buehr, Priscilla Flood
COPY EDITOR
Mary Ann Pfeiffer
Assistants: Joan Rehe, Ruth H. Wolfe

ART DIRECTOR
Irwin Glusker
Associate Art Director: Elton Robinson

ADVISORY BOARD
Gilbert Highet, *Chairman*
Frederick Burkhardt   Oliver Jensen
Marshall B. Davidson   Jotham Johnson
Richard M. Ketchum   John Walker

EUROPEAN CONSULTING EDITOR
J. H. Plumb
Christ's College, Cambridge

EUROPEAN BUREAU
Gertrudis Feliu, *Chief*
11 rue du Bouloi, Paris

HORIZON is published every two months by American Heritage Publishing Co., Inc. Executive and editorial offices: 551 Fifth Ave., New York 17, N.Y. HORIZON welcomes contributions but can assume no responsibility for unsolicited material.

All correspondence about subscriptions should be addressed to: HORIZON Subscription Office, 379 West Center St., Marion, Ohio.

Single Copies: $4.50
Annual Subscriptions: $21.00 in the U.S. & Can.
$22.00 elsewhere

An annual index is published every September, priced at $1. HORIZON is also indexed in the *Readers Guide to Periodical Literature.*

Title registered U.S. Patent Office

Second-class postage paid at New York, N.Y., and at additional mailing offices.

COVER: This golden winged bull, reproduced slightly smaller than its actual eight-inch height, was fashioned by a Persian artist in the fifth century B.C. Though it had been borrowed from the earlier Mesopotamian civilizations, the bull became a favorite symbol of the new, virile kingdom founded by Cyrus the Great. It was worked in gold and other precious metals to evoke the fertility of the flocks; sculptured on stone pillars, it became the warden of the palace gates. For Persia's unique contribution to world culture, as it prepares to celebrate the 2,500th anniversary of the Empire, see page 40.

FRONTISPIECE: Before the French Revolution the Abbey of Saint-Denis possessed one of the most prodigious treasuries in Christendom—six great cupboards full of jeweled reliquaries and sacramental vessels. Among them was this resplendent paten, used to receive the Host during the Eucharist. The central disk of green serpentine is probably Hellenistic (and therefore pagan) in origin; the gold mounting, studded with pearls and precious stones, appears to have been added in the ninth century. The paten came to the newly nationalized Louvre with other church and royal treasures in 1792.

PHOTOGRAPHS COURTESY H. P. KRAUS

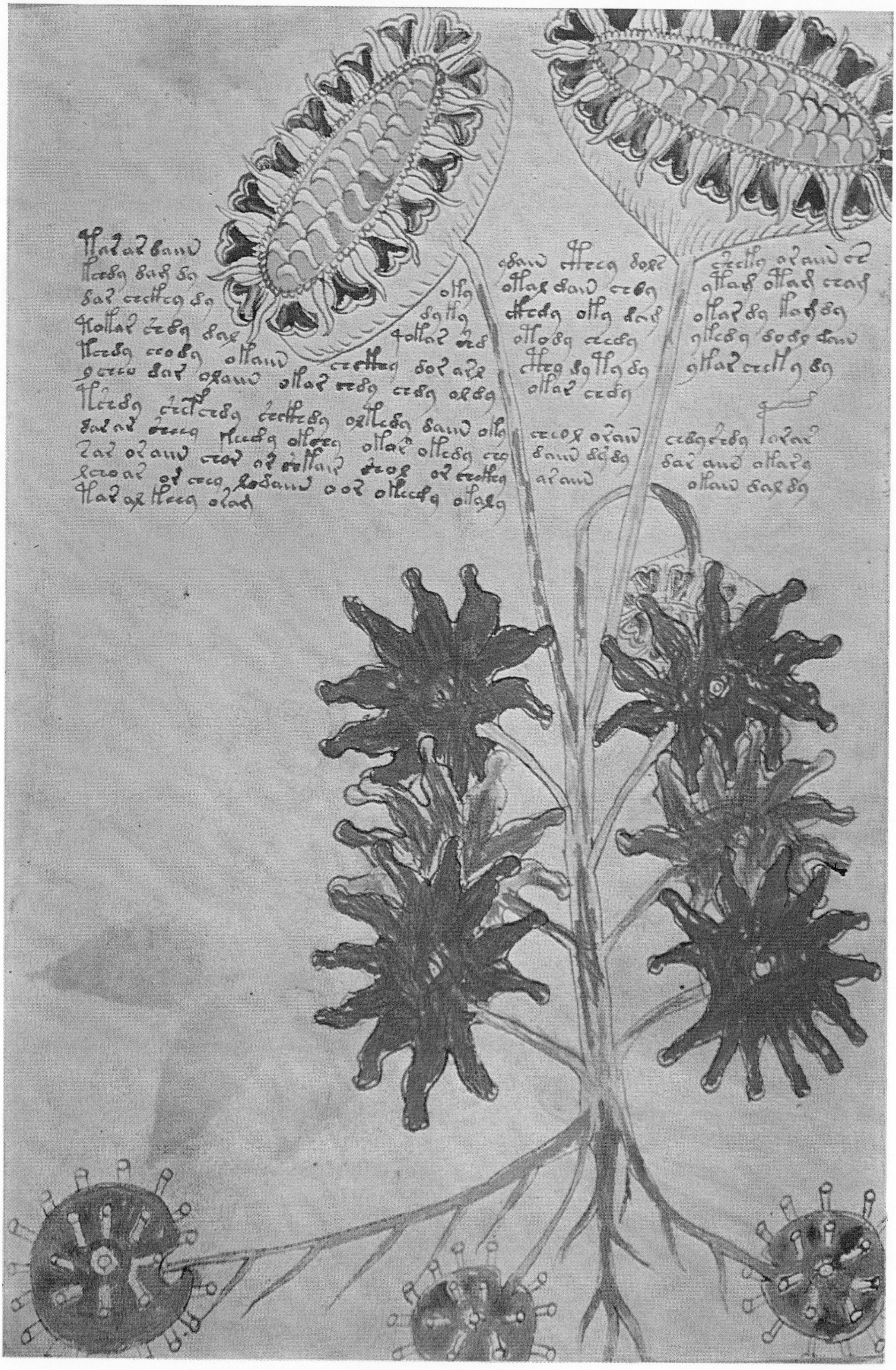

The Most Mysterious Manuscript

Who wrote it, and what is it about? For three centuries its strange alphabet and enigmatic pictures have resisted efforts to decipher it; now a computer will try

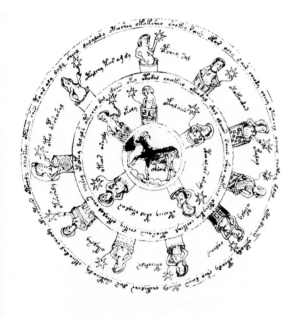

At the center of the drawing above is the sign of Aries, the Ram, so that it is apparently some kind of astrological chart. But who are the little ladies in the tubs? The late William R. Newbold, who thought —mistakenly—that he had solved some of the mysteries of the manuscript, said they represented souls dwelling among the stars. Equally baffling is the strange botanical drawing opposite, which seems convincing enough at first glance but cannot be identified with any known species of plant.

By ALFRED WERNER

Cryptography, the "act or art of writing in secret characters," is mentioned by Roman authors of the first century A.D. as having been used in the time of Julius Caesar, but undoubtedly it dates back much further in origin. For there have always been nonconformists and heretics who had something important to say but could not, or would not, run the risk of having their message read by secular or religious authorities for fear of persecution. Yet these thinkers did not wish to keep their ideas or their knowledge entirely to themselves. Hence it was only logical to devise a code so that they could make their statements in a language that, to the ordinary eye, would cause the manuscript to appear to be the meaningless work of a crank. The author, however, would take steps to make sure that his "subversive" text could be understood by posterity; he might confide the key to unraveling the script to a trustworthy young disciple, or he might—often at the end of the manuscript—insert this key in such a way that it would reveal itself to an earnest student willing to devote countless hours to the task of decipherment. Roger Bacon, the thirteenth-century philosopher and scientist, was such a man.

A particularly fascinating and enigmatic cipher manuscript that some scholars have believed to be the work of Roger Bacon has recently come into the possession of a New York rare-book dealer who values it at $160,000. The firm of H. P. Kraus acquired this centuries-old vellum book (just how old, no one knows) from the estate of Mrs. Wilfrid M. Voynich, widow of the American specialist in rare books who, in 1912, had rediscovered it in a monastery near Rome. Perhaps as much has been

This is almost certainly a page of recipes for potions or pharmaceuticals (note the apothecary jars), but the roots and tubers offer no clues to the text because they cannot be identified. More perplexing is the drawing opposite, which looks like a plumber's dream. It may represent some physiological process, but the salamander and the fish swallowing the woman suggest philosophical overtones as well.

written about it in recent decades as about any other old manuscript. For while the parchment scrolls or codices that we admire in the British Museum, the Bibliothèque Nationale in Paris, or New York's Morgan Library are far more striking in appearance than this manuscript, their texts—in Latin, Greek, Hebrew, Italian, French, or German—offer no major obstacles to the student. In this codex, however, the pages are covered with a secret script that does not even allow us to identify the language in which the message is composed, and with almost five hundred drawings that are equally baffling. One of the scholars who has devoted much time to studying it, the late Professor John M. Manly of the University of Chicago, called it "the most mysterious manuscript in the world."

Physically it is not prepossessing. Its binding is modest. Measuring about nine inches by six inches, it is a small quarto comprising two hundred and forty-six pages of text, of which two hundred and eleven are also illustrated. Turning the pages, one might, on the strength of the somewhat naïve drawings in brownish ink (lightly touched with green, yellow, blue, and dark-red water color), believe it to be a sort of medical treatise; for it superficially resembles other old manuscripts in which plants, roots, and leaves were drawn in because of their medicinal properties. There are also pages of astrological tables that show concentric circles containing suns, moons, and the signs of the zodiac (see page 5), but to anyone who has read Chaucer's *Canterbury Tales*, this will not be inconsistent with a medical treatise: in the Middle Ages a physician was likely to consult the stars for the propitious times to treat patients. The drawings that look like cell structures could belong in the realm of physiology, and the figures of nude women, who seem to be taking baths (see pages 7, 8, and 9), could be related to the sort of hydrotherapy much recommended by medieval practitioners of medicine.

Yet a closer study of the book cautions us that we must not be too hasty in our judgment: just as the writing looks deceptively like post-Gothic Italian cursive script but turns out to be unrelated to any known alphabet, so many of the drawings contain enigmas that have bewildered two generations of twentieth-century scientists and scholars.

Where does this curious little volume come from? The first reference to it is found in a seventeenth-century letter penned in Prague. This was written by Joannes Marcus Marci on August 19, 1666, to accompany the codex, which he was sending as a gift to the Jesuit Athanasius Kircher in Rome. Both the writer of the letter and the recipient were unusual men. Marci, who was physician, mathematician, physicist, and Orientalist in one person, served as rector of the celebrated University of Prague, the oldest school of higher learning in all of Central Europe. In his seventies he joined the Jesuit order. Anticipating the approach of death, he began distributing his own private library among friends. For Kircher, who had been his teacher, he chose the cipher manuscript, convinced, as he said, that it could be read by no one else.

Marci had obtained the book from a friend who had devoted "unflagging toil" toward deciphering the text, but without success. At one time, he wrote Kircher, it had belonged to Emperor Rudolph II, ruler of the Holy Roman Empire from 1576 to 1612, who had paid six hundred ducats for it. The story, though unconfirmed by any documents, is a believable one. The Hapsburg monarch, who passionately collected paintings, built an observatory for Tycho Brahe and Johannes Kepler, and founded a botanical garden, is also known to have acquired a large collection of unusual books.

But where and when did the puzzling attribution of the manuscript to

Roger Bacon originate? In his letter Marci says that a certain Dr. Raphael (who had held positions of importance at the Imperial Court, first under Rudolph II and then under two successors to the throne) had expressed the opinion that the book's author was no less a man than "Roger Bacon, the Englishman." Modestly, Marci claims neutrality in this matter: "On this point I suspend judgment; it is your place to define for us what view we should take thereon."

Father Kircher, famous for his extraordinary interest in hieroglyphs and other archaeological subjects, was a logical choice. But while he has left us three works in which he attempted a solution of the Egyptian hieroglyphs, and also one on codes and ciphers in general, he did not do anything to solve the mystery of this cipher manuscript, so far as we know, nor did he voice any opinions of his own on the attribution to Roger Bacon. Three centuries passed during which no attention was paid to the codex, until Voynich came upon it by sheer accident. He examined and tried to read the text but gave up in despair. It was only in 1919 that he finally sought help from William R. Newbold, Professor of Intellectual and Moral Philosophy at the University of Pennsylvania and an expert in Greek, Latin, and other ancient languages.

Professor Newbold worked heroically on the task of decipherment and died, in 1926, in the belief that he had read correctly at least some sections of the text and that, on the very last page, he had deciphered the author's name, "R. Baconi." So it was, after all, a work of that "Admirable Doctor," one of the most extraordinary figures of thirteenth-century Christian Europe! Indeed, whenever a mysterious manuscript has turned up, it has always been a scholar's immediate inclination to attribute it to Bacon, that English Leonardo who, though a devout member of the Franciscan order, had the kind of inquisitive mind that brought him into conflict with his superiors. "The end of all true philosophy is to arrive at a knowledge of the Creator through knowledge of the external world," Friar Bacon maintained, proclaiming the indispensability of experimentation. So even if the text of the cipher manuscript defied modern scholars, did not the drawings suggest the authorship of a man who had made discoveries so extraordinary as to bring him under suspicion as a delver in the black arts?

As for cryptography, Friar Bacon, in one of his works, specifically deals with the means by which the learned can hide their secrets in ciphers. He held the opinion that the man who had succeeded in penetrating one of nature's secrets had, as it were, been taken into God's confidence, and should therefore not be so sacrilegious as to reveal to the vulgar the fruits of his labors. Besides, toward the end of his life his books were condemned by the head of the Franciscan order, and he was thrown into prison. Was it not quite likely that, as a prisoner, Bacon would resort to cryptography to thwart the authorities who had forbidden him to continue his studies? Could he not have given the completed manuscript to a favored disciple, along with the key to its decipherment?

These thoughts must have stimulated the imaginative mind of Professor Newbold who, knowing that his hero had also had visions of horseless carriages, motorboats, and flying machines, and was even credited with the invention of gunpowder, did not stop short of making him the greatest inventor of all time. For, from Professor Newbold's posthumously published work *The Cipher of Roger Bacon* (Philadelphia, 1928), Roger emerged as a man who possessed both a telescope and a microscope, which he had constructed himself and which enabled him to fathom many secrets of astronomy and of microbiology that

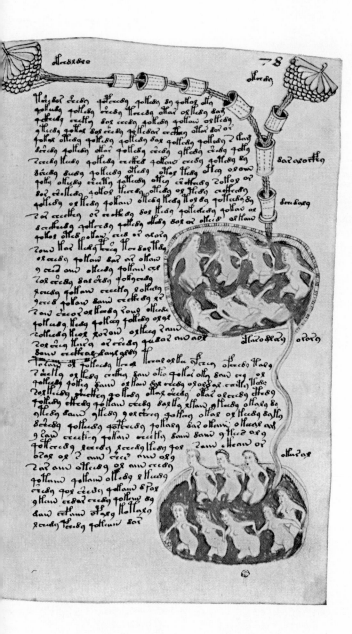

Newbold saw this as a drawing of the generative process, which may be right—even though scholars no longer accept his accompanying assertions that the manuscript was by the thirteenth-century philosopher and scientist Roger Bacon, and that Bacon must have invented the microscope.

were to remain hidden from the rest of mankind for several centuries.

Newbold's astonishing claims, though, were demolished by several scholars who refused to accept any one of them and even went so far as to deny that he had deciphered a single word in the manuscript. Yet much damage was done, for the results of his researches were accepted, all too naïvely, by a number of handbooks. To indicate how far a dedicated scholar can go in self-delusion, it might be added that Newbold, with the aid of the alphabet he derived from the manuscript's last page, read into the text a reference to certain riots that took place in Oxford when the serfs left their masters to flee to the monasteries, as well as instructions for the production of metallic copper. Newbold even thought he had found a statement in the manuscript to the effect that Pope Clement IV was suffering from "stone in the bladder," had asked Bacon for help, and had been given medical and surgical advice.

Today all of Newbold's findings have been rejected. Upon one thing all scholars agree: the manuscript cannot have come from the hand of the thirteenth-century Englishman Bacon, even though future research may still prove it to be a *copy* of a work by him. Everything—including the quality of the vellum, the nature of the drawings, and the character of the script—indicates that the manuscript was produced close to 1500, at least two hundred years after the Friar's death. It is also quite certain that text and drawings were made by the same hand. But who the writer was, and in what language the hidden text was written, no one yet knows.

Since we cannot read the text, we must concentrate on the drawings, which are large and well preserved but not the work of a trained illuminator. The vast majority—nearly four fifths of them—depict plants or the sections of plants. Do we, then, have before us a herbal? Herbals have existed since antiquity, the most famous being *De Materia Medica,* the compendium of plants and animals by Dioscorides, the great pharmacist of the first century A.D. Dealing with the healing power of animals and plants, it had a great vogue in the Middle Ages.

Like *De Materia Medica* this manuscript shows plants and next to them, or below them, what could be scientific commentaries. But whereas in most ancient or medieval herbals the plants are botanically recognizable, in this instance many of the drawings appear to be conventionalized or stylized beyond recognition. As a matter of fact, only sixteen plants among about four hundred botanical drawings have been tentatively identified by experts. Some of the remaining plants are composites (the root system belongs to one plant, the stem system to another, the leaves and flowers to still others), while others show purely imaginary root or flower structures. Did the scribe, who apparently was identical with the draftsman, deliberately and consciously offer "free" versions in order to conceal something—just as the cipher is a cover-up for a text still unknown to us?

While everything—including what appears to be a pharmacist's mortar and pestle—makes this book look like a herbal, this semblance may be little more than crafty camouflage. Germans who lived under the Hitler regime remember books with the most innocent-looking title pages and equally unpolitical first two or three pages that, after further examination, turned out to be violently worded anti-Nazi tracts. Did the flowers and plants serve a similar purpose of misleading the authorities and of diverting their attention from the curious cryptography?

There is no explanation for the countless nude females who turn up in the concentric circles of what are certainly the signs of the zodiac, and in other "biological" drawings (on a single page there may be, in two or three sections of the book, as many as twenty or even thirty of these lively but rather obese little ladies, who seem to be taking baths). Professor Newbold ventured to see them as symbols for the life-creating process, leading from the sperm to the ovum and to the embryo. Another learned man endeavored to link these figures to the ancient Greek physician Galen's "vital spirits," which—according to the Stoic philosophy—come from the stars and are drawn with the air into the body, where they initiate and sustain all vital functions. Some of the nude ladies (there does not appear to be a single male in the illustrations) are ensconced in barrel-like objects—bringing to one scholar's mind the *Gorgias* of Plato, in which the philosopher compares the body to a "leaky cask" that the soul occupying it must continuously labor to keep full of food, drink, and warmth. Astonishing, too, are the drawings that look like infinitesimally tiny sections of plant organisms, as if the medieval author had observed them through a microscope (which, we are reasonably sure, was not invented before the end of the sixteenth century).

Among the latest experts to have given attention to the cipher manuscript is Colonel William F. Friedman, America's leading military cryptologist. Unhappy about the fact that no more is known of the manuscript beyond what was known to Marci three hundred years ago, Colonel Friedman decided to stir up interest among a group of scientists at the Radio Corporation of America who were engaged in research and analysis in the field of information systems. RCA has offered him the use of free time on one of its modern computers. All the words of the manuscript are being transcribed on separate cards to be sorted and counted and possibly interpreted with the help of the machine.

It is not impossible that one day such research will bear fruit. One of the letters penned by England's unhappy King Charles I—who, like his wife, was adept in the use of ciphers—was not deciphered till two centuries after the King was beheaded. But it is also conceivable that the cipher manuscript will never yield up its secrets. This would be a pity, for it can be said with certainty that the book is not the meaningless work of a crank. Something indefinable about it leads us to believe that its author—whether or not his name was Roger Bacon—was a serious philosopher who, with all the scientific and philosophical means at the disposal of a man of his era, was trying to find a way to grasp the significance of the cosmos in which man lives, half-blind yet always with the earnest hope of seeing the light at last.

Alfred Werner is a contributing editor of Arts Magazine. *He wrote the article on the Vatican in the January, 1962, issue of* HORIZON.

As these details show, the hand that made the drawings was not that of a practiced artist—but it was guided by a sharply observant eye. The little ladies are drawn in the postures of everyday life, and with such vividness that the mystery of their function becomes all the more frustrating.

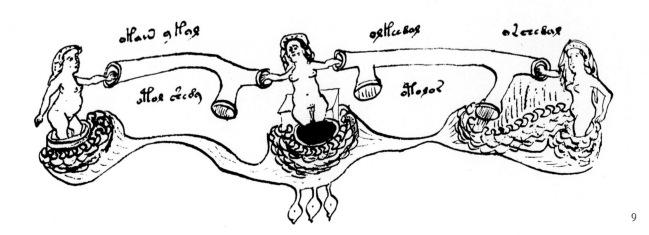

BOSTON CHOOSES THE FUTURE

By ERIC LARRABEE

*For its new City Hall, it held an open competition.
The winning design is bold, unorthodox,
and a good omen for American architecture*

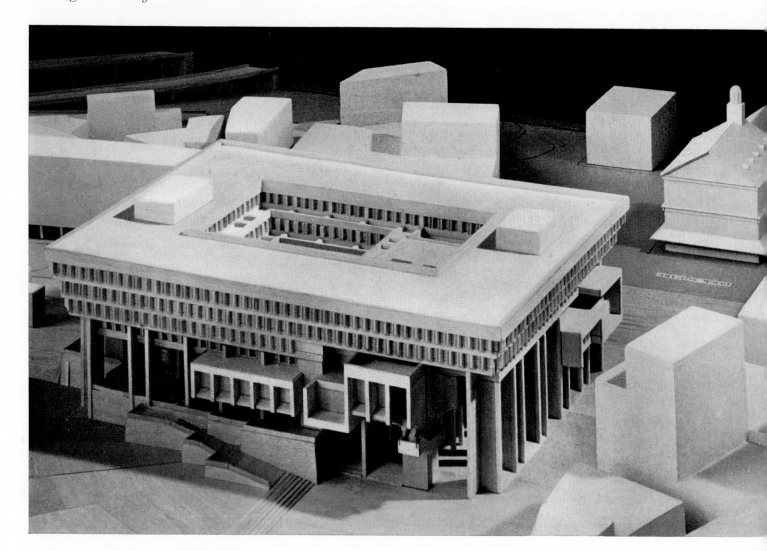

The city of Boston, hub of the universe and home of the Last Hurrah, has been in its time a building-conscious community. Monuments to its architectural enterprise and finesse—like H. H. Richardson's Trinity Church or McKim, Mead, White's Public Library—still stand, amid the decay of its Downtown into stretches of obsolescence interrupted by large, modern banalities. Not far from the Church and the Library, however, in a light and airy office newly opened, twenty or thirty young men are busily designing a shape and a symbol for a new Boston, one that should deserve as well of posterity as the older Boston deserves of us.

They are the architects (plus associates and draftsmen) of the new Boston City Hall. They were chosen by open competition and, until they won it, they were virtually unknown in the architectural profession. Their design (see the model opposite) is original, not to say daring, and considerably different from what one has come to expect of American governmental building at home—a style that ranges roughly from WPA Post-Office Colonial to Neo-Fascist Federal.* Their dream is going to be realized because a city, hitherto anything but notorious

*See "Lifting the Federal Façade" in HORIZON for January, 1960.

for civic incorruptibility, determined to do the right thing and, more important still, to carry through on it. This is the first open competition for a major American municipal structure to be held in almost sixty years. The example Boston has set, as the architect Percival Goodman has written, "could be a turning point in American architecture."

The winners are three New Yorkers: Gerhard M. Kallmann, Noel Michael McKinnell, and Edward F. Knowles. Kallmann (German-born, now in his forties) and McKinnell (English-born, in his twenties) were both teaching at Columbia University and were not "practicing" architects, in the technical sense of the term, when they decided to enter the competition; they asked Knowles, as a registered architect, to join with them. Since being awarded the commission, they have received outpourings of praise: the sagelike Walter Gropius says their building "has a beautiful scheme." It is all heady wine to them. They are shy, hopeful, and very busy.

Open competition is far from the normal method by which architectural commissions are awarded. Generally a client, for a stated fee, will ask a limited number of architects to submit

An early sketch (see below) for the new building (model at left, including Faneuil Hall) shows how the graded angles of the plaza and open access to an inner court were anticipated by the designers (right): Gerhard Kallmann at left, Michael McKinnell at right, and assistant Gordon Tully at center.

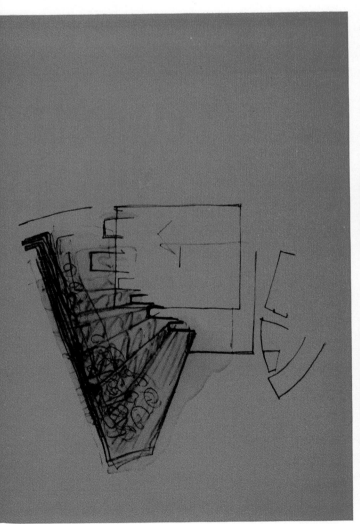

preliminary sketches, and then he will make a choice among them on whatever criteria he pleases. Architects are professionals in the sense that, like doctors and lawyers, they are forbidden to advertise or to solicit work. Therefore their profession tends toward oligarchy. The well-known architects become still better known; the big firms get the big jobs.

Opening a competition to all comers is the obvious way to break the circle of the select, but the history of architectural competitions has not been uniformly encouraging in this respect. It is littered with the bones of aborted victories and unjustified defeats. The winner may get the prize but not the job or, more likely still, one of the also-rans may turn out to have had the superior design. Grant La Farge in 1891 won the competition for the Cathedral of St. John the Divine only to lose it some years later, in a controversy of considerable bitterness, to Ralph Adams Cram. In 1922 Raymond Hood won the Chicago *Tribune* competition with the Gothic tower it now occupies, although Gropius submitted a far more forward-looking design (see below), and Eliel Saarinen—the brilliant father of a famous son, Eero—came in second with a late entry which,

even though it lost, virtually made his reputation in America. Most memorable of all, Le Corbusier entered the competition for a new palace of the League of Nations in 1927, with a plan so challenging and intelligent that the judges had to award nine first prizes—and then turn the final decision over to the politicians—in order to avoid giving first place to Corbusier's trailblazing building.

This makes it all the more remarkable that the Boston competition has had a happy ending. This near-miracle can be attributed in part to the courage of Mayor John F. Collins, in part to the energetic Government Center Commission, and in part to the leading architects of Boston, who apparently extended themselves to make it clear to city officials how important this particular commission was. The City Hall will be the central element, the kingpin, in a vast multimillion-dollar project for a new Government Center—involving five subways, an arterial highway, commercial properties, a Federal office building, and a sizable motor hotel—in the neighborhood of Faneuil Hall and Scollay Square. The City Hall is to sit in the middle of a wide plaza, the visual and psychological center

The history of competitions has often been unhappy. Gropius's design for the Chicago Tribune *(below left) was far more enterprising than Raymond Hood's (below right), which won, while Corbusier's losing plan for the League of Nations (next below) was mocked by the winning marble mausoleum (bottom).*

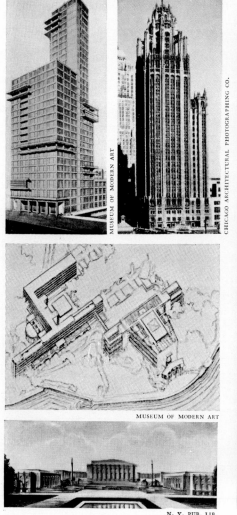

MUSEUM OF MODERN ART

CHICAGO ARCHITECTURAL PHOTOGRAPHING CO.

MUSEUM OF MODERN ART

N. Y. PUB. LIB.

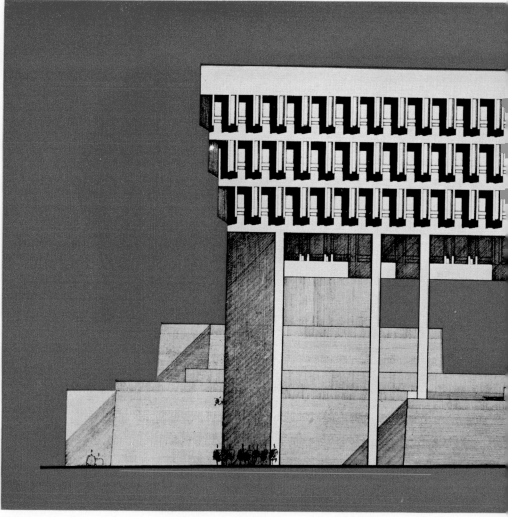

of attention. If the City Hall plan went wrong, as the architects could see, everything else would go wrong, too.

A contest of this kind, since it attracts wide attention, commands the best efforts of both the big and little operators. There were 256 contestants, more than forty of them established architects. On the jury were three businessmen, as well as four architects of stature and experience: William W. Wurster, Walter A. Netsch, Ralph Rapson, and Pietro Belluschi. The results, in terms of the balance between notable and obscure practitioners, were astonishing. The eight finalists were all relative unknowns. Of the thirty-four designs chosen for public exhibit, fewer than ten were by well-known firms. And the winners, as we have seen, were absolute underdogs. If proof were needed that there exists in this country an enormous reservoir of untapped architectural talent, that proof had been provided.

Kallmann, McKinnell, and Knowles won unanimously on the first ballot. What made their building so compelling, in architects' terms, is that it had "solved" the problem—that is to say, it had reconciled and fulfilled the requirements of the program both spatially and structurally. What the architect is supposed to combine, in the practice of his craft, are his knowledge of construction and practicality, his three-dimensional imagination and his aesthetic judgment. Most buildings don't even try; some show the effects of a last-minute effort to rescue them from mediocrity; the great ones bear the mark of sound conception from the start. Here the mark was visible, and the jury knew it when they saw it.

There exists a preliminary sketch that Kallmann and McKinnell made the day they had lunch together and decided to compete. It is a remarkable foreshadowing of their final plan: from the very beginning they appear to have realized that they would have to open the building up to let space, air, and the public in. When they first looked at the "cubage" the City Hall required (that is, the number of cubic feet its necessary interior functions would consume), they saw that a normal building of such a size would visually be far too small; it would be swallowed up in the vastness of the plaza. They knew they would have to explode it, pull it apart—"aerate" is the word they use. Fortunately this was what they wanted to do any-

The City Hall's west façade (below) shows the sharp contrasts between the ramps and balconies of the moundlike brick base, the vigorously indented shapes surrounding the windows of the city council chamber at mid-level, and propped above them the cast-concrete fins of the top three office floors.

how. "We wanted people to feel that this was their building," Kallmann has said. "We wanted them to be drawn in." All well and good; the only problem for the designers was what they were going to do with their pulled-apart spaces.

The City Hall of Boston has three major constituent parts. The first is a set of bureaus that deal directly and continually with the public in large numbers—the place where you go to get your auto license renewed, and the like. The second is office space for pure bureaucracy, which doesn't have to be as accessible as the first. The third is ceremonial, a cluster of three elements embodying the dignity and power of the city: a library, the city council chamber, and the mayor's office. The architects put the public bureaus in a massive, tapered brick base (they call it "the mound"). The out-of-the-way offices they raised in the air on concrete pillars in a kind of upside-down Mayan pyramid of slotted, precast concrete providing a maximum of uniform quarters open to the view. The ceremonial elements they arranged in the space between, around high hallways and a central courtyard, in a complex jigsaw puzzle of interrelated spaces. The ingenuity of this interlocking compelled the jury's admiration, and makes the building work.

In appearance the new Boston City Hall belongs to the tradition shaped by Le Corbusier and best epitomized, in this country, by Louis Kahn.* It is a style of strong and angular forms in plain, rough concrete, which respond closely to their functions and achieve elegance—or beauty, if you will—through the severe, Spartan purity of their design. The budget at Boston was low, which oddly enough the architects welcomed, since it stimulated them to make the most of rough materials. In opening up the building's interior, making it easy to move in and out of, they aimed for a quality suitable to civic ceremonial, both imposing and inviting—a quality Kallmann calls "democratic monumentality."

Obviously, a building cannot be fully visualized from its plans, nor will it necessarily come out looking exactly like them. But if the Boston City Hall lives up to its promise, it will be an even more impressive structure in actuality than it is in anticipation. The blueprints cannot show, for example, the color contrast that will come from the difference between the red brick of the base and the light, precast concrete of the

*See "Architect's Hero: Louis Kahn" in HORIZON for September, 1962.

Lifted bodily in the air off its base, as in the three-dimensional cutaway drawing below, the Boston City Hall would reveal the complicated jigsaw-puzzle pattern of its courtyard, main hallways, and important civic spaces—such as the mayor's office (top) and the city council chamber (left corner).

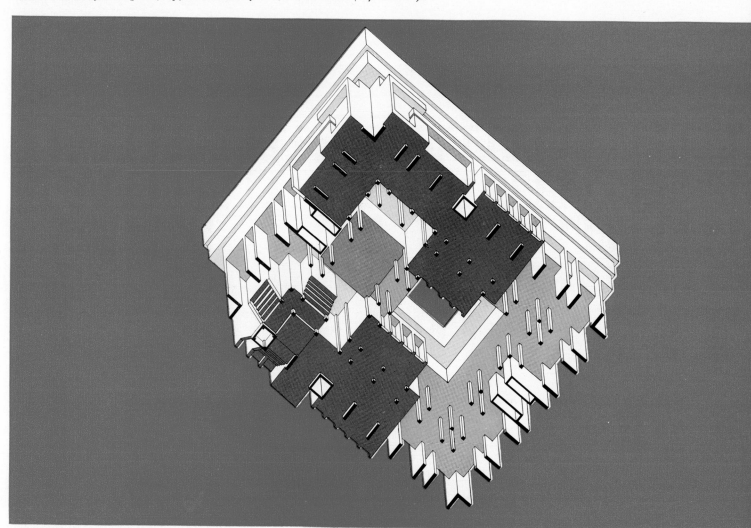

offices above. Even renderings in perspective can do no more than suggest the rhythm of changing patterns and volumes that will emerge as one walks the halls and climbs the stairs. It should be an interesting building to move around in, which is perhaps the most generous gift an architect can bestow.

But one of the unique qualities of the Boston City Hall is that so many of them are already visible in the plans and model. It is a remarkably *comprehensible* building. You can see what it is doing, and why. It will stand, furthermore, as an example of how a certain kind of modern architect thinks. Looking at it one can say: this is what this kind of architecture is about—richness of conception, severity of form, high intelligence and art in combining them.

Kallmann and McKinnell hope that their success will encourage the use of competitions elsewhere, and will encourage the far-from-universal practice of abiding by the jury's decision, once it has been made. Objections to competitions are often heard: they are wasteful, they do not guarantee good results, they are expensive, the inexperienced may win. But what, as Percival Goodman has asked, is the guarantee of good results by any method? In Europe most selections are made by competition and the results are in no way inferior, in fact the opposite. As for the wasted effort, architects enter the contests willingly; they often spend just as much time and effort, under the existing system, on buildings that do not get built. As for the expense, says Goodman, "for something less than $60,000 Boston secured preliminary designs that surely would have cost half a million dollars had they been commissioned in the normal way."

Boston's jury, in any event, has turned in a decisive verdict that will stand for some time as a model of responsible civic conduct. The jury also, in so doing, summed up its estimate of the winning design, and this too could be a model of aware judgment and clear exposition. "At a distance," they said, "the building achieves great monumentality, drama, and unity; and in detail the contrasting textures, the play of light and shade, the richness of forms and spaces, culminate in a series of dramatic terraces which provide a strong focus for the symbol of city government. It is a daring yet classical architectural statement, contained within a vigorous, unified form."

Openness extends to the interior ceremonial spaces (below, in sketch, with their deep grille ceiling), an effect some of the also-ran designs (at right) sought each in their way to achieve, by trying to become (top) a coliseum, (middle) a steel-and-glass box, or (bottom) what might be the Globe Theatre.

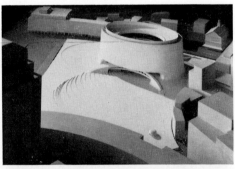

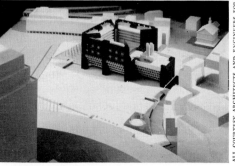

By IRWIN GLUSKER

WHAT NEXT IN ART?

Now that abstract expressionism is the established "Academy," a new crop of painters is striking into a brave new world of bulls-eyes, mock advertisements, jigsaw cutouts, and colored-up hardware

Loyalties in art, though fierce, are curiously inconstant. Today even its best friends are turning with indecent haste from the rapidly cooling corpse of abstract expressionism, not to write obituaries, but to find a successor. Actually, this search is not new; it has been apparent for several years that a new wave of artists, growing restive under the dominant style of the past decade, was seeking an expression of its own.

The death of Jackson Pollock in 1956 found the newly ascendant abstract expressionists almost totally victorious, but with a major leader fallen. While less dramatic in its circumstances, the passing of Franz Kline last year at the age of fifty-one—not old, not young—brought the realization that abstract expressionism no longer represented the Revolution, but the Establishment. The *enfants terribles* of the late forties and of the fifties had established themselves as the Academy, with all its perquisites of international acclaim, museum status, and even a limited Philistine acceptance, as well as refreshingly handsome remuneration for the members.

A large number of significantly differing painters were huddled together under this spattered, squeegeed, and explosively colored abstract-expressionist tent. The movement was also called, rather parochially, "The New York School" and, even less accurately, "action" painting. Such painters as Pollock,

Kline, Willem de Kooning, and Jack Tworkov can indeed be classified as "action" painters—artists whose work derives its impact more from the energy of the gesture and the expressive power of the paint itself than from the forms for which paint has traditionally been the vehicle.

Grouped with them, however, were equally significant artists whose styles are based on a more controlled handling of medium and image, represented—quickly—by Mark Rothko, Adolph Gottlieb, and Robert Motherwell. The success of their intent depends on the concentration and distillation—the abstraction, if you will—of symbols or motifs to their greatest and most telling intensity.

But to classify these two groups of artists as exclusively "painterly" or "imagist" is to overlook the richness inherent in a mixture of means. There are, in both groups, those who take a direction between these poles. The impact of a Kline is part "paint" and part "structure," while the evocative forms in a Motherwell depend to some extent on the excitement of "paint" for their effectiveness.

These painters, now mostly in their fifties, represent the shore upon which the new wave began to break. But it seemed to come from several directions. Some of these efforts had taken shape during the most productive years of abstract expression-

TEXT CONTINUED ON PAGE 25

16

Kenneth Noland, "Noon Afloat" (1962, 48″ x 48″). Now thirty-eight and living in New York City, Noland paints weightless, geometric canvases that are perhaps not as simple as they look: after the initial visual punch, his circles, targets, and pinwheels are seen to rotate, flare outward like solar eclipses, or expand like the ripples from a pebble tossed into water.

Above: Marcia Marcus, "Double Portrait" (1962, 68″ x 78″). The much-heralded return of figure painting has brought to the fore a group of younger American artists who paint the figure in a flat, unmodeled, cutout style that may be pre-Renaissance but also looks crisp and new. Miss Marcus, who is thirty-four, finds her most convenient models at home: her family and friends. The painting above combines a self-portrait with one of her husband in an antique bathing suit.

Opposite: Jasper Johns, "Fool's House" (1962, 72″ x 36″). Ever since his first one-man show in 1958, Johns has been known for paintings that depict or actually incorporate flags, targets, numerals, letters, and man-made objects—anything, in fact, but man himself (when he appears, it is only in the form of dead plaster casts of living flesh). Here Johns simply hangs a castoff broom onto his canvas. At the age of thirty-two he has plenty of time to push his strange quest further.

Overleaf: Ellsworth Kelly, "Green on Blue" (1962, 82″ x 68″). Kelly's sharp outlines, flat colors, and simple shapes are typical of what has come to be known as the "hard-edge" style, described by one critic as seeking "to combine classical control with powerful color or shape sensation." Though still abstract, it is a definite reaction against the seething tangles of abstract expressionism. Kelly, thirty-nine, spent six years in Paris after the war, and now lives in New York.

On page 21: Al Leslie, "The Iron Picture" (1961, 108″ x 72″). One of the most aggressive "action" painters of the fifties, Leslie now seems to be turning in a different direction: straight lines and rectangles have moved in among the drips and spatters of his earlier canvases. Though the painting's title gives no clue, it may seem jazzily evocative of the verve and violence of New York, where Leslie was born, grew up, and—at thirty-five—still lives and paints wall-sized pictures.

19

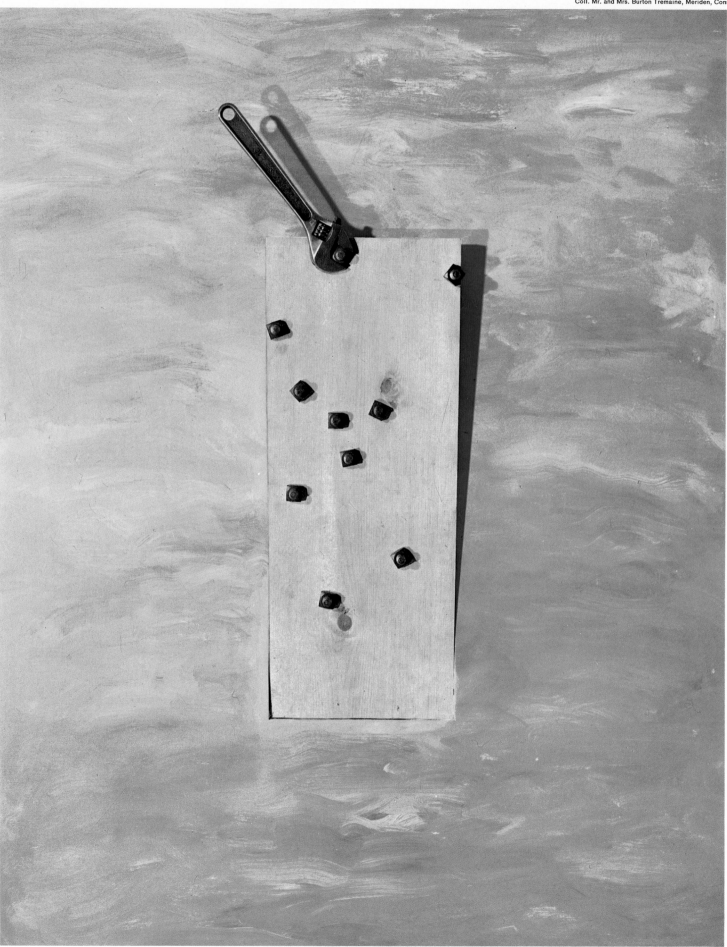

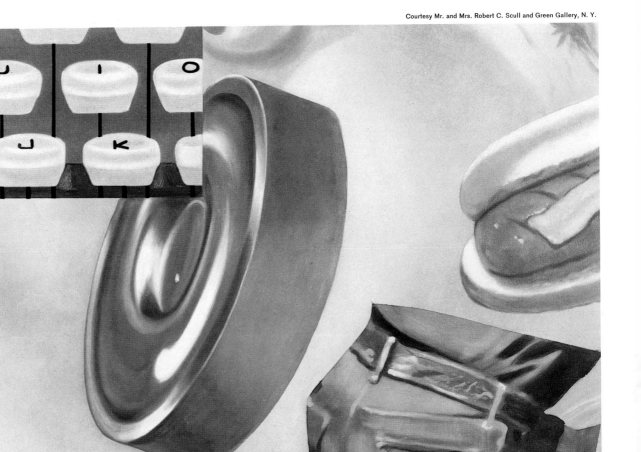

Opposite: Jim Dine, "Crescent Wrench" (1962, 60" x 50"). Dine used to put real neckties in his compositions, then real tools—as here—and also soap dishes, sinks, lawn mowers, anything. Because he has wit, the results are often quite funny. But Dine is apparently aiming for something more than that: he disclaims any intent to shock, and says he only wants to make paintings that are "direct and immediate like a sign." When he succeeds, the results are quite handsome.

Above: James Rosenquist, "The Lines Were Etched Deeply on the Map of Her Face" (1962, 72" x 96"). This new "pop" artist, who once painted billboards for a living, says he thinks of the face simply as geography (look at a billboard face close up) and of the other images as "associations" hovering over it. Here he combines typewriter keys, a Life Saver, a pair of workmen's jeans, and a hot dog, with the profile of a woman — vastly enlarged — in the background.

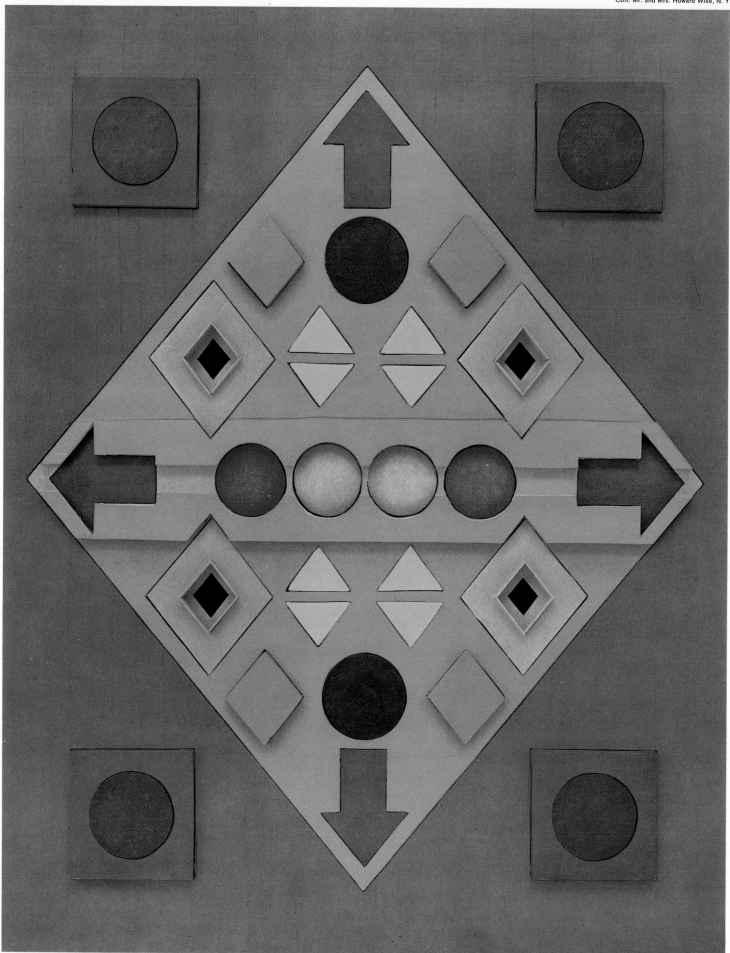

George Ortman, "Blue Diamond" (1961, 60" x 48"). A game, a puzzle, a mocking traffic sign? It might be any of these, or it might not; the thirty-six-year-old artist says only that he is "a symbolist and a maker of signs" (that word again). In his reliefs of wood and painted canvas the visual language of streets and highways and pinball games is stripped of its conventional meaning and rearranged to make what might be called escutcheons for the machine age.

TEXT CONTINUED FROM PAGE 16

ism; others are barely old enough to have been named by their critical godparents. But two broad groupings are discernible among those painters who are trying to find a way forward from abstract expressionism. One is intent on rarefying, controlling, and classicizing the abstract idiom, and its approach is variously described as "hard-edge" or "abstract imagist." The other is clearly searching for a new expression of the world in which all of us live. Rejecting the abstract, they are employing the mass-produced images, ideas, and even artifacts of our assembly-line civilization. Whether the result is called the New Realism or, less misleadingly, "pop art," it is a mistake to think that these painters herald a return to nineteenth-century representation as such. Reality has undergone a curious alchemy once again, and the world of appearances is still available to us only in the private transformations of the artists.

The geometry of Kenneth Noland's paintings—his circles, targets, crosses—are the vehicles for a visual experience having nothing, or very little, to do with subject (page 17). The means employed are almost completely formal—relying on optic play and visceral reaction to shape and color. This approach, classically abstract, is shared by other painters including the late Morris Louis, a friend and neighbor of Noland's when they lived in Washington, D.C.

The viewer seeking reassurance from the familiar enjoys a very short-lived comfort even in the most conventionally realistic of recent approaches. The images employed by Marcia Marcus (page 18) are easily understood—people, flowers, interiors. Yet even in her work the figure is related to its environment in original and exciting ways. These painters use the figure for improvisation, as a jazz pianist might use an old tune. The juggling of perspectives and unlikely juxtapositions of techniques (minuscule detail in one area, broad painting in another) give to the unexceptional a new edge, to the obvious a new presence, and to the tired a new force.

Even as abstract expressionism, under full steam in the mid-fifties, reveled in violent color and dazzling virtuoso exercises in paint, a quieter and more introspective approach was being shaped. The early Jasper Johns paintings of flags and targets, some rimmed with boxed plaster faces and casts of anatomical fragments, were among the first of this genre. The very commonplaceness of the subjects chosen by Johns brought the viewer face to face with the utterly familiar, but new in terms of how Johns saw it. The critic Leo Steinberg has suggested that Johns no longer uses paint as a medium of transformation. For him, a painting must be what it represents: because the picture plane is flat, the only things that can be painted without make-believe are those which are flat by nature; if he wants to include something that is three-dimensional, he fixes the object itself to the canvas—as in the case of the broom on page 19.

The work of Ellsworth Kelly (page 20), along with that of Leon Polk Smith and others, represents a romantic kind of geometric abstraction. Using a hard, clean edge to define expressive, counteracting shapes, Kelly's colors are related in

tense equilibrium. While his works run to some size—and size is a very telling element in much of this new work—they are modest in dimension compared to the nine-foot-high canvases of Al Leslie.

Leslie's paintings (page 21) combine the discipline of the geometrician with the explosive paint handling of the "action" painter. At thirty-five he is considered a member of the "second generation" of the New York School, making him closer kin to the abstract expressionists than any of the other painters in this portfolio.

Jim Dine, at twenty-seven, and James Rosenquist, twenty-eight, are the youngest of the artists represented here. Along with Claes Oldenburg, Wayne Thiebaud, Roy Lichtenstein, and Andy Warhol, among others, they are probably the most prominent of the New Realists. Although these painters do not work together as a movement, they all use in various ways elements of our everyday environment as the subject of their work.

The Dine painting (or is it a construction?) on page 22 is one of a series he has done on tools—not painted representations, but the real thing placed on canvas. He uses them because he thinks they are beautiful, not as examples of industrial design, but as "useful, familiar things having to do with people."

Rosenquist draws on his experience as a billboard painter in using banal, familiar, but hitherto unrelated images brought up very close and very large. The background in the painting reproduced on page 23, for example, is a grotesquely enlarged detail of a woman's face. The juxtaposed elements of typewriter keys, a green Life Saver, and a man's blue jeans interact to render the parts unfamiliar and, hopefully, to make fresh commentary on our commercialized society.

For George Ortman, a Californian now resident in New York, the surface of a painting is not a plane to be kept intact. Squares, diamonds, circles, all sorts of signlike shapes, are cut out of that plane, painted, resurfaced, and then replaced. Contrasts of texture are as important as those of color, and the total magic of Ortman's conjurings with emblems is greater than the sum of his very rational means (opposite).

Abundantly varied as are the samplings of current effort illustrated here, they may be broken down into the historic duality of the classic and the romantic. The Nolands, the Kellys, and the Ortmans may be observed as answering their need to impose order and formalize their reactions to experience and to the problem of painting itself. The others may be seen as expressing themselves more with ideas and imagination, with paint itself a less important element in the equation of expression. There is, of course, a whole spectrum of mixtures of these several approaches.

One final point is to be made here: the return to "reality," which was so hopefully heralded a year or two ago by those who hold to the pendulum theory of art, is hardly affirmed by these artists. What they borrow from the "real" world is transformed, redefined, and redirected. The kaleidoscope of contemporary painting may have tumbled for a moment into a realistic configuration—but in this art, strange are the uses of reality.

By IRVING WARDLE

One of the Royal Court Theatre's most scathing new plays is Chips with Everything, *Arnold Wesker's blast at the way of life of the Royal Air Fo*

Six years ago Arthur Miller accused the British theatre of being "hermetically sealed off from life," and this was no unjust accusation. London's stages had become an animated social museum, with an appeal rather like that of the Tower or the Tussaud Waxworks. Audiences sat watching gilded replicas of themselves in spacious country-house settings, woodenly exchanging small talk and confronting every shock that life or pulp fiction had to offer with imperturbable good breeding. In short, the West End theatre was a backwater, totally cut off from the revolutionary ferment boiling up off Broadway and on the Continent.

This picture is no longer accurate. The past half-decade has seen the eruption of a movement that has shaken up the British theatre as a whole, from the avant-garde outposts to the central citadels of conservative taste. The prime mover in this upheaval has been an organization called the English Stage Company, which was set up seven years ago with the main purpose of attracting good writing into the theatre. What the English Stage Company has done since is to bring forward a string of adventurous new playwrights (among them John Osborne, Harold Pinter, Arnold Wesker, John Arden, and N. F. Simpson) and new theatre directors (Tony Richardson, John Dexter, William Gaskill, John Blatchley, Lindsay Anderson, and others). The Company has persistently challenged "Aunt Edna" (as Terence Rattigan has called her), that previously unquestioned arbiter of West End taste, by reopening the great question, "Is entertainment enough?"

The formation of the Company is an ironic chapter in theatre history, for it was originally intended as a platform for poetic drama—a genre that promptly went into eclipse once the Company was installed. The idea was hatched by three men: Lord Harewood (now Director of the Edinburgh Festival), J. E. Blacksell (a Devon schoolmaster), and the poet Ronald Duncan.

A backer was found in the person of Neville Blond, a Yorkshire textile magnate. The next need was for an artistic director—and here the choice fell on the actor and teacher George Devine, who had begun his acting career in 1932 and had rarely been away from the profession for long, but had managed to remain aloof from the world of the West End. Instinctively cosmopolitan, he saw London against a Continental horizon, and was painfully aware that box office rules forbade anything like the avant-garde productions which minor German playhouses were able to put on with the aid of municipal subsidies. The great influence in Devine's life was Michel Saint-Denis, with whom he had worked at the legendary London Theatre Studio, the Compagnie des Quinze, and later at the Old Vic Theatre School.

After the war and the closure of the Old Vic School, Devine had found himself less than ever in sympathy with the state of

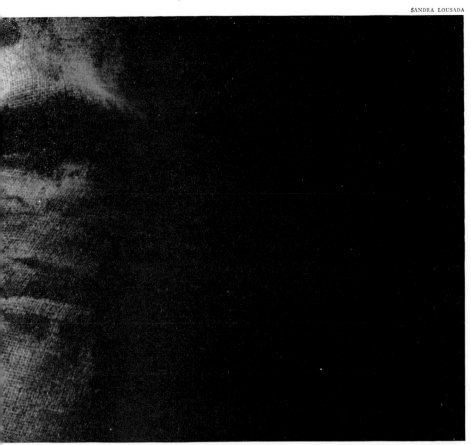

At London's Royal Court Theatre a company of young rebels has broken with a genteel tradition in the name of defiant realism and experiment

Revolt Against the West End

above: a recruit is forced to bayonet a sandbag dummy in what, for an airman, is senseless drill

the British stage; he felt that the only effective means of opposing the "system" was by running an organization of his own—either a school or a theatre with the artistic policy under his control. In collaboration with a young ex-Oxford television director, Tony Richardson, he had in fact drawn up a scheme for such a theatre. And so it came about that the Royal Court, a theatre with a history of music hall, cinema conversion, intimate revues, and bomb damage, with a seating capacity of 480, a useful forestage, and the most exasperatingly squeaky auditorium in London, became the house of British living drama.

Before the English Stage Company got under way with its first show, it soberly promised "to present new British and foreign plays in repertory seasons; to arrange simply mounted Sunday productions of promising work by newcomers, both writers and producers; and to regard high standards of dialogue and performance as more important than extravagant décor and production foibles." Devine added: "It is easy to see modern painting and hear contemporary music in London, but there is no theatre where one can be sure of seeing a contemporary play." The moment was propitious. Critics welcomed the scheme rapturously, and articles on "writers' theatre" blossomed on every arts page.

What was needed was a stockpile of new drama. But this was a problem since serious playwriting in the English theatre was almost extinct. And no wonder: whatever the prizes of a suc-

cessful West End run, these were thoroughly offset by the conditions of the trade—interminable delays in the reading of manuscripts, delays in casting, mutilation of the script by the star or director, the danger of withdrawal during a provincial tour, the long wait for a vacant house in the West End, and above all, the indifference of commercial managements to the quality of a work. Not surprisingly, English writers had quietly turned their backs on the stage and applied themselves to the less frustrating worlds of fiction and poetry.

Devine was bombarded with new plays when the production plans were announced, but after reading and rejecting nearly seven hundred of them he declared: "The main fault with all the plays I've read is that what they have to say has nothing at all to do with life as we live it today." If he were to get new material, he concluded, it would have to come from established sources. Continental authors wrote plays as readily as novels—why couldn't well-known English authors be induced to do the same thing? Accordingly he approached the novelists Angus Wilson and Nigel Dennis, both of whom agreed, and the program for the first three months was drawn up. It opened with Wilson's *The Mulberry Bush;* the other plays were Arthur Miller's *The Crucible,* a double bill by Ronald Duncan, *Don Juan* and *The Death of Satan,* Nigel Dennis's adaptation of his novel *Cards of Identity,* and—the only contribution from an unknown writer—John Osborne's *Look Back in Anger.*

27

The guiding spirit of the Royal Court Theatre, George Devine (top), manages, produces, and on occasion directs and also acts—as in Samuel Beckett's Endgame. *His assistant, Tony Richardson (bottom), is best known as the director of plays or films written by John Osborne: among them,* The Entertainer, Luther, *and* Tom Jones.

The discovery of Osborne is the most momentous event in the E.S.C.'s history, but the enormous success of his work cut in two directions: it saved the Company financially, but it also led to the identification of the Royal Court's policy with Osborne's violent Left Wing antagonisms—a considerable embarrassment to the more conservative members of the council.

However, *Look Back in Anger* certainly satisfied Devine's demand for drama about life in modern Britain. The unprepared first-night audience sat through a ferocious onslaught on the Monarchy, the Church, and the middle class, delivered almost uninterruptedly by a single character. Jimmy Porter was the prototype of the Angry Young Man—a working-class university boy who has withdrawn in disgust from the success race and dived into an ostentatiously squalid existence, flourishing like a Welfare State Timon of Athens.

We can now see that there is much more in the play than straightforward social polemic. On another level it is a study of how a marriage can go wrong when the husband has more energy than the wife. And Jimmy, although he is allowed to trample on the other characters, is anything but an idealized spokesman for the author; on the contrary, he virtually demands to be regarded as a louse. Like Osborne's other heroes, he has a compulsive need to antagonize the audience, and his idiom is one of violent (and un-English) emotion; sometimes the result is dramatically powerful, sometimes shrilly foolish.

But for the first audiences what mattered was the play's social impact, almost unequaled in the British theatre. I sat next to an icy and immaculate woman who kept up an obbligato of outraged gasps till the moment when Jimmy's face is slapped, at which she spat out: "Well, thank God somebody has done that at last!"

As for the play's supporters, their admiration was not far short of ecstasy: what they saw was the first full-scale portrait of a man they all knew, but who hitherto had exercised scarcely any public voice—let alone a voice in the theatre. The great phalanx of disenchanted ex-university boys, becalmed in the smugly apathetic life of postwar Britain and swallowing their gall in minor teaching jobs and industrial training schemes, found a spokesman of corrosive brilliance in Jimmy Porter, and some of his embattled phrases (such as the "chinless wonder from Sandhurst") went straight into the language. The idiom was full of bitter comedy, implacably suspicious of all institutions, including marriage, and finding its only point of emotional stability in jazz. A familiar tongue, but one not heard in the theatre before.

When the manuscript of *Look Back in Anger* reached Devine, it had already done the rounds of the London agents. Osborne, an impoverished actor living on a Chiswick houseboat, sent the play to the E.S.C. as a last resort. Devine records that the dialogue "leapt off the page," and he knew he had to do it.

It is worth recalling the objections raised by agents at that time to the manuscript, for they reveal something of the gulf separating today's English taste from that of six years ago. One agent referred Osborne to a newspaper article deploring "the tendency amongst modern playwrights . . . to disregard the necessity of telling a story in terms of the theatre." Another sent back the manuscript, commenting that the plot was exaggerated and the characterization disagreeable. A third complained that the play "lacked theatrical effect and shape" and that it "would not stand up to stage representation"; this reader also took a violent dislike to the hero, Jimmy Porter—"He is just another neurotic who has not had the courage to take in his stride the youthful shocks and sufferings that most people experience."

These strictures—echoed subsequently by the older critics—already sound dated; the conception in England of dramatic character and plot has undergone severe changes. Nowadays it is unreasonable to talk about "just another neurotic" without inspecting the particular neurosis; and as for plot—what does the word mean? It used to mean a skeleton underlying the other elements of dialogue and characterization—the chassis of the dramatic vehicle. In that sense—the sense intended by the middle-aged journeymen who had held a monopoly on British playwriting—none of the young English writers of the past few years is a plot man. As in car production, the chassis has given way to the stressed skin—the vital elements tend nowadays to reveal themselves in the surface tension of the writing.

However, neither *Look Back* nor the other plays in the Court's first season caused an immediate rush at the box office. For the first nine weeks audiences hovered below half capacity, in spite of Kenneth Tynan's famous outburst in *The Observer* in which he called *Look Back in Anger* the best young play of the decade and swore he could not love anyone who remained indifferent to it. Then, in the ninth week, a short extract from the play was televised. Instantly the box office was besieged, the telephone continuously busy, and within three days there were four sacks of mail demanding tickets.

Despite the runaway success on his hands, Devine tried to persist with a repertory system. Nigel Dennis's *Cards of Identity* entered the program in June—and returns fell off considerably. Even so, the scheme might have survived had it not been for the ill-fated next play—an elaborate production of Bertolt Brecht's *The Good Woman of Setzuan,* which calamitously coincided with the Hungarian Revolution. The year of Suez and Hungary was one in which the British public, for once, awoke from its political torpor; this was a great advantage to Osborne, but for the Communist Brecht, it spelled disaster. Devine, who played in the production, says that never in his career has he experienced such withering hostility from an audience; and the production was withdrawn with heavy losses. This in effect was the end of the repertory.

The Company recouped some of its losses by reviving *Look Back,* and by putting on one of the bawdiest of all Restoration comedies, William Wycherley's *The Country Wife,* which transferred to the West End and made a handsome profit. Devine was to go on experimenting with repertory in a desultory way for another year or so; but to all intents and purposes, the Court was now like any other theatre in that it gave plays uninterrupted runs and engaged fresh casts for each production. Devine recently summed up the situation in these words:

In order to survive we have been forced to participate in the commercial jungle, subject to the normal commercial risks. A "bad press" and down we go. Apart from about a thousand people there is no regular public to support us through thick and thin. To pay our way we have to achieve "rave notices." It is this kind of climate which drives people . . . out of the theatre.

But the English Stage Company was not driven out of the theatre. It did not go to the lengths suggested by Kenneth Tynan, who said it ought to pay for experimental shows by putting on nude revues, but it did exploit properties like Noël Coward's *Look After Lulu* and Dudley Fitts's sexually supercharged version of Aristophanes' *Lysistrata.* Under cover of such money-spinners it set out to enlarge its scope, not only in full-dress public productions, but in a whole network of subsidiary activities that made it a workshop as well as a theatre. New writers were put under option and given free passes to rehearsals; public discussions were held after performances, and forums on writing arranged; assistant directors were taken on staff; and new plays were given try-out performances—"productions without décor"—on Sunday evenings.

In themselves, these tactics would have accomplished nothing; but, by a stunning stroke of fortune, they happened to coincide with the first real boom in English playwriting since the Restoration. This has now slackened off, but at the time there was a seemingly inexhaustible outpouring of new talent in the wake of Osborne. A mass of scripts in the "angry" style were received, and rejected by the Royal Court; but the material that actually reached the stage had nothing in common with *Look Back in Anger.* All the authors owed to Osborne was the demonstration that there was now a place in the theatre for good modern writing. And the variety of the work they produced defeats any attempt to classify it as a school. The writers themselves were of equally diverse origins, some (like Osborne) coming from the working class, others being firmly settled middle-class professionals; some Jewish, some West Indian; some under twenty, and some over forty; even some already in the theatre. The only thing they had in common was their remoteness from the conventional theatre world.

The first major discovery after Osborne was N. F. Simpson, a middle-aged teacher who belongs to the tradition of English nonsense writing, his particular forte being the rigorous pursuit of logical absurdities and *non sequiturs.* In *A Resounding Tinkle* a pair of suburbanites wish to return their captive elephant to the zoo in exchange for a snake; discovering the snake is too short for a cigar box, the husband suggests having it stretched, to which his wife objects, "Ah, yes; but then you'd lose the thickness." Simpson's plays take no social or moral line, but what does come through is an exposure of middle-class proneness to cliché and readiness to get used to anything. He himself is a gentle, shy man who uses his hands a great deal to fill in the gaps in his conversation. There is nothing facile about him, and writing is a slow, painstaking exercise. What he possesses is an unerring comic instinct, as William Gaskill, the director of his plays, testifies:

TEXT CONTINUED ON PAGE 32

Harold Pinter

John Arden

John Osborne

Arnold Wesker

N. F. Simpson

Ann Jellicoe

Postwar drama in England has taken its main impetus from the Royal Court Theatre playwrights, who have encompassed a surprising range of subject matter and style. Harold Pinter's eerie The Caretaker, The Dumbwaiter, and The Birthday Party, which have been called "abstract thrillers," present characters in conflict but without apparent motives. The dialogue and the themes of John Arden's plays are not bleak like Pinter's; ranging from comedy (The Happy Haven) to tragedy (Serjeant Musgrave's Dance), they have a richly poetic quality. Arnold Wesker, whose Trilogy deals with the fortunes of a Jewish family in London from the 1930's to the present, has dedicated himself to a theatre aimed at improving the condition and stimulating the cultural awareness of working-class people. By contrast, N. F. Simpson insists that his plays (A Resounding Tinkle, One-Way Pendulum) are fantasies with no social implications whatever. John Osborne, "the first Angry Young Man," has consistently assailed sacrosanct British institutions—from the Press (in his musical The World of Paul Slickey) to the Royal Family; while Ann Jellicoe writes sympathetically (in The Sport of My Mad Mother and The Knack) about the experiences of free-living teen-agers. The work of these and other Royal Court dramatists, played—and imitated—in America as elsewhere, has broken with old formulas to provide broader definitions of what constitutes an interesting play.

His knowledge of timing is extraordinary. For him, it's a kind of systematization of something that comedians have always known. But whereas they usually say, "Wait for the laugh," Simpson says, "You won't *get* the laugh if you don't wait before delivering the line." . . . To Simpson it is a sort of scientific process: the audience laugh even when they don't want to.

Ann Jellicoe is a professional theatre worker (among other things, she has run her own group, the Cockpit Theatre), but the play that made her name, *The Sport of My Mad Mother,* slips into no accepted dramatic category. It is a rhapsodic study of a teen-age London gang, led by a girl who is identified with the Hindu goddess of destruction, Kali. The writing is closer to Eliot's fragment *Sweeney Agonistes* than to anything else, but what Miss Jellicoe really set out to do was to create poetry from the rhythms of gang speech—much the same thing that Jerome Robbins carried out with gang movement in *West Side Story.* Now in her thirties, Ann Jellicoe has the looks of an extremely handsome tomboy, and a burningly serious manner. She is more group-minded than most of the new writers, but her latest play, *The Knack*—a coolly poised study of the techniques of seduction—suggests she is the most boldly experimental of all.

Another writer the Court has promoted in the teeth of critical dismissal is John Arden,* an architect turned playwright, whose plays have explored so many styles that one might wonder whether several men were writing under his name. What explodes this suspicion is the consistency of Arden's language—a muscular, compressed instrument with echoes of the Jacobean dramatists and the Border Ballads; for all its literary quality it is as real as a lump of earth. His plays have dealt with the collision between respectable citizens and social outcasts (*Live Like Pigs*), with bloodthirsty religious pacifism (*Serjeant Musgrave's Dance*), and with life in an old folks' home (*The Happy Haven*). And in these three plays he has rung the changes of modern realism, period fantasy, and grotesque comedy. He is a powerful and extraordinary writer, but one who has only slowly gained recognition; without the Royal Court he would probably never have found it.

Arnold Wesker and Harold Pinter cannot properly be classed as Royal Court discoveries; they arrived there having already made their reputations. Both are Jewish, both are pacifists, and both come from the working class of London's East End. But there all resemblance between them comes to an end. Wesker is an ardent Socialist who now runs an organization called Centre 42 with the aim of bringing culture to the workers through trade-union backing. Pinter acknowledges no political alignment and resists anything that looks in the least like group pressure; like Samuel Beckett, the author he most admires and resembles, he is simply an artist, and it is one of the ironies of the theatrical boom that he should have bypassed the period of dedicated obscurity of the minority writer and become a popular success.

Arnold Wesker, before his work aroused attention, had an itinerant life. After early Zionist aspirations in the Habonim movement, he went into the Royal Air Force and subsequently

worked as a farm laborer and a pastry cook. These experiences form the basis of his main work, *The Wesker Trilogy,* three plays that trace the ideological pilgrimage of a London Jewish family from the 1930's up to the present day. American spectators might compare it unfavorably with Odets and their other prewar social dramatists, but it has made a powerful impression on British critics; and Wesker's latest play, *Chips With Everything,* has at last brought him large audiences.

There is no such identity between life and art in Pinter, who is a brusque, convivial ex-actor with the appearance, somebody has said, of "a go-ahead Charing Cross Road shirt salesman." His work, as anyone who saw *The Caretaker* on Broadway will know, is theatrical poetry; he creates a dark world of his own from the disregarded fragments of common life, and at its best, his dialogue is a distillation of Cockney speech patterns into something that can move one as music does.

These are only some of the names that have come to light since the Royal Court began; there are many others—the marvelously imaginative eighteen-year-old Michael Hastings; the novelists Doris Lessing and Kathleen Sully; the actor-dramatist Alun Owen; the West Indians Barry Reckord and Errol John; Nigel Dennis, a mandarin satirist who would have been at home in the literary twenties. In this situation, the Court's Sunday night "productions without décor" have been vital in providing an outlet for plays that could not be given a full-scale run.

The extraordinary thing about the Court's Sunday night shows is the permanent mark many of them left on the public memory. Not many people saw Michael Hastings's *Yes—And After,* or John Arden's *The Waters of Babylon,* or the financially disastrous one-week run of *The Sport of My Mad Mother.* And yet these events are now widely agreed to have been landmarks in the theatre of the fifties. The most striking example is *Serjeant Musgrave's Dance,* which was largely dismissed by the critics and ignored by the public but has since acquired a towering reputation. As Devine laconically remarks: "*Serjeant Musgrave's Dance* is now an O.K. play (they are studying it in schools), even if it did lose us a cool £5,820 in 1959."

The diversity of the English material and the quantity of French and American drama in the programs ought long ago to have squashed the myth that the English Stage Company is a hotbed of doctrinaire Socialism and a stronghold of the Angry Young Man cult. It is neither. Its working-class writers have been in the minority; and the famed "redbrick," or provincial, actors who came to prominence at the Court before going on to conquer the West End and the film industry were never a dominating influence in the Company.

However, the myth has persisted, even though the personal tastes of both Devine and Richardson lay much more in the direction of lyrical and romantic theatre (to begin with, they were distinctly resistant to the committed Left Wing plays of Arnold Wesker). One reason for the continued reputation of the Court as a center of political axe-grinding is the paradox that the greatest commercial successes were still Left Wing plays—Osborne's music-hall tour de force *The Entertainer,* with its excoriation of English tradition, and Willis Hall's *The Long and the Short and the Tall,* a popular antiwar play in the "angry" manner; also the Court's first musical, *The Lily White Boys,* a facile Brechtian pastiche on the theme of "property is theft."

In a shadowy way the Court still retains this reputation for political commitment, but no one nowadays suspects it of harboring bomb throwers on the premises. In one way this is a pity, for there is no doubt that the Court is no longer as exciting a place as it was in its first two years when the political consciousness of the country was aroused to such a degree that Osborne in *The Entertainer* was able, without impropriety, to refer to Trafalgar Square rallies and Lieutenant Moorhouse's death in Egypt during the Suez crisis.

What remains is a somewhat nebulous devotion to good writing on modern themes; and because—as Sartre recently remarked—a good Right Wing play is an impossibility, what political emphasis there is continues to be Socialist. But the Company is at the mercy of what its authors choose to submit. If N. F. Simpson supplies a play, the public will be in for another dose of topsy-turvy nonsense logic in the manner of a latter-day Lewis Carroll; if the author is Arnold Wesker, the theatre will temporarily become a platform for manifestoes on the class war.

The English Stage Company's present position is thus hard to define. The climate of taste has changed profoundly, but the big managements are still in power and as ready as ever to buy up rebellion and exploit it as fashion: it is a familiar process, known in England as "Harrodization" after the modish Knightsbridge store, Harrods.

Pioneering advances in the modern theatre have generally been the work of permanent or semipermanent groups—the Moscow Art Theatre, the Berliner Ensemble, the Israeli Habima Theatre. The English Stage Company is not such a group, nor does it possess the resources to become one. But it has two great assets: it is fashionable enough to entice star players to work at a fraction of their normal salary; and although there is no fixed company, there is a large pool of actors who have developed a strong sense of loyalty from working there and are always ready to go back for another show. There have been occasions when a team of these regulars has come together in a production to constitute a true ensemble. This happened in William Gaskill's production of Arden's comedy about senility, *The Happy Haven,* which was played in masks and took on the mimetic brilliance of *commedia dell' arte*—a style one tends to regard as beyond the range of British actors.

Devine's next aim is to acquire a West End theatre and to install successful shows in the center of town while retaining the Court as a basis for experiment and cohesive training. If this dream comes true, then the Company may indeed escape from what he calls "the commercial jungle" and develop into the kind of powerful, independent force that brings about lasting revolutions.

Irving Wardle, a London theatre critic for The Observer *and* Encore, *has reviewed many of the Royal Court productions.*

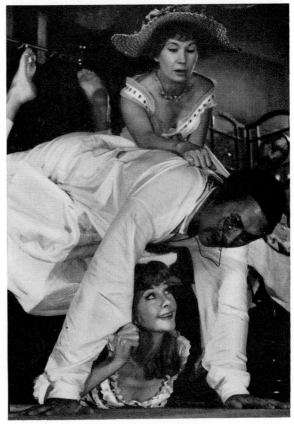

When the Royal Court Theatre produced Look Back in Anger, *its author John Osborne was an unknown quantity; so was the youthful Company itself, which included Mary Ure and Kenneth Haigh as the outspoken Jimmy Porter (top) who, in one reviewer's words, "did not so much act as explode." Later the Court drew such famous performers as Vivian Leigh, who wriggled under beds (bottom) and slammed doors, in* Look After Lulu, *Noël Coward's version of the classic French farce by Georges Feydeau.*

AN APOLOGY FOR GLUTTONS

By PATRICK LEIGH FERMOR

The hazards of gluttony are well known: what is still to be reckoned is its marvelous influence on history

"Gluttony. Yes. Let me see." Mr. Vortigern paused in the pillared doorway to light a cigar, and his ruminative murmur was punctuated by puffs.

"*Voracitas* . . . Γαστριμαργια . . . *Gola* . . . *Gourmandise* . . . Yes. . . ." His cigar properly alight, he sailed down the steps to the sunlit street in an aromatic cloud. No one would have thought this hale, elegant figure was seventy-five.

"I have been a martyr to it, in a mild way, all my life," he resumed as we headed for St. James's Palace. "So its presence among the Seven Deadly Sins has always bothered me. There's nothing against good living in itself. We have only to remember the Marriage at Cana. Saint Benedict allowed his monks a *hemina* of wine with their meals. And look at the distilling traditions of the monastic orders. There has always been a port-drinking, Horace-quoting tradition in Anglican cathedral closes, and all those paintings of cardinals clinking glasses must be founded on something.

"What are the five ways of sinning by gluttony . . . ? *Praepropere, laute, nimis, ardenter, studiose?*" Mr. Vortigern ticked them off on his fingers. "Too soon, too expensively, too much, too eagerly, and making too much of a fuss. . . . Too much and too eagerly are the worst. I shudder to think of myself as a boy, reeling from the table stunned with toad-in-the-hole and sausages and mash and jelly and spotted dog, and steeped in sin.

"Mercifully, a glimmer of moderation came with riper years. For, now that Science has disarmed Lust of its retaliatory powers, Gluttony is the only one of the Deadly Seven which is visited by physical retribution this side of the tomb. . . . It is the only sin which turns us into monsters.

"The Germans are the worst, for sheer bulk. What miles of liver sausage, what oceans of beer and quagmires of those colossal bellies! How appalling they look from behind; the terrible creases of fat three deep across solid and shaven napes! Necks wreathed in smiles, the stigmata of damnation; and delusive smiles, for when they turn round there is nothing but a blank stare and a jigsaw of fencing scars.

"The outward effects of food are a sure guide. In England they are very noticeable. Prosperous Edwardians had an unmistakable ptarmigan sheen. There was beef and claret in the faces of the squirearchy, cabbage and strong Indian tea among nonconformists, and limpid blue eyes in the Navy, due to Plymouth gin, and so on. Above all, a general look of low spirits that tells its own tale. Direct results are still more striking. Curry induces instability of temper and fosters discord; hot Mexican food leads to cruelty, just as surely as blubber, the staple of the Eskimos, spells torpid indifference. The rancid oil they cook with in Spain tastes as though it came straight out of a sanctuary lamp; no wonder the country is prone to bigotry. And those extraordinary gray complexions of the Americans I attribute entirely to breakfast foods, jumbo steaks, soft drinks, milk shakes and ice cream at all hours, washed down by conditioned air and crooning."

Mr. Vortigern's words had brought us to the Mall. We crossed into the park and he smoked thoughtfully for a minute. "The most convincing example of the influence of food on national character is Italy. Look at Italian art. Pasta wrecked it! Some say it was imported from the Orient by Marco Polo. Others that an old woman discovered it in Naples in the time of Frederick II of Hohenstaufen, the *stupor mundi*. I favor the second theory. Cimabue and Giotto and Duccio lived on dried fish and polenta and beans and black bread and olives. And you can't picture Dante eating spaghetti, or Amico di Sandro wolfing ravioli down. They lived on hardtack from the *trecento* to the Renaissance, you mark my words.

"Then *pasta asciutta* came. It must have taken a century or two to conquer Italy, spreading from the south like a clammy and many-tentacled monster, smothering Italy's genius on its northward journey, and strangling its artists like the serpents of Laocoön. Thousands of seething and dripping tongues of macaroni squirming and coiling up the Apennines, gathering volume every mile, engulfing towns and provinces and slowly subduing the whole peninsula. The North held out heroically for a while—there is no pasta in those banquets of Veronese—and the last stand was at Venice. The rest of the country lay inert under its warm and slippery bonds—slippery, perhaps, but still unbroken today—while Tiepolo held out, and Longhi and Guardi and Canaletto, the last lonely frontiersmen of a fallen Empire.

"But one day some treacherous dauber must have swallowed a streaming green yard or two of *tagliatelle*—the end of the enemy's foremost tentacle, you might say—and, hotfoot, the rest of the huge, victorious monster came coiling into the Veneto and reared itself for the kill. And then"—the end of Mr. Vortigern's Malacca cane, which had been describing faster and faster loops in the air, stopped in mid-sweep—"and then, wallop! A billion boiling tons of pasta fell on the town, and the proud city, the sea's bride, with her towers and domes and bridges and monuments and canals, went under. The piazzas were a tragic squirming tangle of spaghetti and lasagne, the lagoon ran red with tomato sauce. Italy's genius was dead, laid low by her own gluttony . . . not only Italy's painting, but Italian thought and poetry and literature . . . and even Italian architecture. Everything was turned into macaroni."

Mr. Vortigern fell silent. The world seemed locked for a while in an elegiac hush. "But," he resumed at last, "it had its compensations. Baroque's debt to pasta has never been fully recognized. In fountain statuary its influence was supreme. Think of those beautiful fountains at the Villa d'Este and Bagnaia! Think of the Piazza Navona and the Piazza di Trevi! Where do you think they found the inspiration for all those bearded Tritons, those Neptunes and gushing river-gods and sea beasts, those swirling beards and fish tails and manes, all ending in waterweed? That feeling for tempestuous and tangled flow, of deliquescence, of solidity in flux, that *brio* and speed and sweep?

"Where but in those swirling ingurgitated forkloads, those wild mealtime furlongs that keep a Roman going? They are pure Bernini, an Italian dinner played backwards, Gorgon-struck, in mid-swoop. . . . Conversely, how eatable post-Renaissance Italian architecture looks—scagliola rock cakes, Carrara barley sugar, marzipan statuary, pasta in travertine, ceilings and cloudbursts straight out of an icing gun! It is not for nothing that the Victor Emmanuel monument is called the Wedding Cake. Perhaps," Mr. Vortigern continued with a change of key, "one should adopt a gastronomic approach to all architecture. The Taj Mahal would be delicious, especially on a hot day. Gothic horrible; too bony. And I would not care for a square meal of Corbusier, either. Too square by half and far too austere. The food might be concrete, I feel, and the drink abstract. . . .

"France, you will agree, is the place where the instinct has been most successfully harnessed and exploited. But this pre-eminence exacts a cruel price. The liver! That is their Achilles heel! It is a national scourge, brought on by those delicious sauces, by all those truffles and chopped mushrooms peeping through the liquid beige. Every Frenchman over fifty writhes under its torments. He is a chained Prometheus, a victim of the tribal inventiveness. Only it's no vulture that pecks at the weak spot but the phantom and vengeful beaks of an army of geese from Strasbourg."

Mr. Vortigern broke off. We paused on the Regent's bridge while he lit a new cigar. "It is odd," he resumed, "that *solid* gluttony has inspired so small a literature—outside cookery books, I mean—compared to its liquid form. There is Rabelais, of course, and the 'Eloge de la Gourmandise,' and that amazing Norman guzzling in Flaubert, and there must be more. Des Esseintes's black banquet in Huysmans doesn't really count: it was aesthetic, and gastronomic. But there is no end to poems in praise of wine. Hundreds of them! Those beautiful similes! Wines that steal up to one like shy fawns, and other delightful comparisons! They are charming! Charming, but hopeless. These writers face the same problem as mystics attempting to convey their experiences in the language of profane love."

He watched a pelican preening its breast feathers for a moment. "What a pity the same device is so seldom used in a derogatory sense: Algerian that charges like a rhinoceros, port-types that draw alongside like charabancs, liqueurs that reek like a bombed scent factory! Yes, blame, as well as praise, should be codified. Michelin allots stars for merit, and rightly. We follow them across France like voracious Magi. Vortigern's Guide would have them, too, but also a scale of conventional signs to warn my readers. A bicarbonate pill first, then a basin, a stretcher, an ambulance and, finally, a tombstone.

"Or perhaps, in extreme cases, a skull and crossbones: robbery and extortion as well as poisoning. For these malefactors are the true sinners. They, and the criminal accomplices who swallow their wicked handiwork without a murmur. These accessories after the fact are guilty of a far greater sin than gluttony." Mr. Vortigern's voice had assumed a sepulchral note. "I refer to Despair.

"Surely it is not casuistry to say that neglect of the fruits of the earth is doubting divine providence? Why do sturgeons swim in the Volga? Why do trout glitter and dart? What makes oysters assemble at Colchester and plovers lay their forbidden eggs? Why do turtles doze in the Seychelles and crustaceans change their carapaces and mushrooms rise from their dunghills and truffles lead sunless lives in Périgord, and grouse dwell in the Pictish mists? Why do strawberries ripen and why do vine tendrils grow in those suggestive corkscrews? Why is the snail on the thorn? Is it to test us or is it a kindly providence at work? But the Fathers have spoken. It's no good trying to shift the blame or to say that sin lies only in excess. How can one eat caviar in moderation? There is another peculiar thing about gluttony: its physical penalties may be the heaviest, but it is the sin that leaves us with the lightest deposit of guilt. One feels like Saint Augustine—of Hippo, not Canterbury—postponing his reformation. 'Give me frugality and sobriety, Oh Lord,' one might paraphrase him, 'but not yet.' *Sed noli modo!* But it's no good. Cerberus and the hailstones are waiting." Big Ben chimed its preliminary tune and began to toll the hour.

"There," Mr. Vortigern said, "is the note of doom. I must go. . . . The time for emendation of life grows shorter. And the time for further backsliding too. . . . *Sed noli modo! Sed noli modo!*" His voice had regained its wonted buoyancy and his eyes were akindle. "Are you free this evening? Capital. Come to me at eight o'clock. Don't be late. I won't tell you what we are going to have, but I think you will like it. The condemned men will eat a hearty dinner."

Of English-Irish descent, Mr. Leigh Fermor is a perennial wanderer of Europe and an original writer about it, at home especially in innermost Greece, as described in his book Mani.

In Print: JOHN BARTH

"Twenty-five years ago," John O'Hara once wrote, "it was delightful to find a writer who would come right out and say Locomobile instead of high-powered motor car, Shanley's instead of gay cabaret and George instead of François, the *chasseur* at the Paris Ritz. These touches guaranteed that the writer knew what he was talking about." It is going on twenty years since O'Hara wrote these words, and there are novelists around today who know not Locomobile nor Shanley's nor their modern equivalents, nor care. They lack, demonstrably, O'Hara's infatuation with reportage, but they possess something else—a "sense of fantastic-ness, an astonishment at life." The speaker is John Barth.

Barth, who is one of our few genuinely serious comic writers, believes that American literature is moving "away from realism and toward plot, contrivance and invention, the sort of thing we haven't seen in our fiction since Hawthorne." Modern physics, for one, has made us aware that "reality is more preposterous than realism—wilder and less plausible." Furthermore, "there are deep metaphysical reasons why we need more Fielding-like books today, with plots where everybody turns out to be related to everybody else." Fielding, yes, and Cervantes, Sterne, Boccaccio, Machado de Assis—all of them authors Barth admires. The adjectives he applies to John Lyly's *Euphues* define the admiration: "His dialogue is preposterous and contrived; the book is full of amazing coincidences, intricate conceits, enormous extravaganzas."

Consider *The Sot-Weed Factor*, Barth's third novel. It has for its hero one Ebenezer Cooke, a "rangy, gangling flitch" who pronounces himself "*Virgin*, sir! *Poet*, sir! Not a man, but Mankind!" Ebenezer seeks a way to "leap astride of life"—and finds it in a commission to write an epic poem titled the *Marylandiad*. The Laureate embarks from London for Colonial Maryland—and Barth sets in motion a plot of Byzantine complexity in which no man is what he seems and in which poor, tattered reality is so magnified, refracted, distorted in the multiple mirrors of the hero's mind, that he at last seeks tranquility in the life of a sot-weed factor, or tobacco peddler. The chapter headings do not adequately suggest Barth's extravagance (he devotes seven pages to summoning 228 synonyms for "whore"), but they imply some of his bawdiness of manner and ironic intent: "In His Efforts to Get to the Bottom of Things the Laureate Comes Within Sight of Malden, but So Far From Arriving There, Nearly Falls Into the Stars"; "The Laureate Indites A Quatrain and Fouls His Breeches"; "Mary Mungummory Poses the Question, Does Essential Savagery Lurk Beneath the Skin of Civilization, or Does Essential Civilization Lurk Beneath the Skin of Savagery?—but Does Not Answer It."

Disguise, ambiguity, illusion. ("In a sense," reads the opening line of Barth's second novel, "I am Jacob Horner.") And with these, something else: "In my first three novels," says Barth, "it was my intention to speak about nihilism, which innocently I felt to be my own discovery; I ended by speaking instead of innocence, which had discovered me." The first of his novels, *The Floating Opera*, is about a small-town lawyer in the Chesapeake tidewater country who realizes with "dumb, stunned surprise" one morning that "this day I will make my last": he will commit suicide on a showboat, "Adam's Original & Unparalleled Floating Opera." The second, *The End of the Road*, is about an English instructor, one Jacob Horner—"at the same time giant and dwarf, plenum and vacuum, and admirable and contemptible"—whose lack of a moral center withers the lives around him and leads to the death of his pregnant mistress at the hands of a quack Negro doctor.

Both novels derive their energy from their flawed heroes —men who are constitutionally unable to feel or act but who invite action, even violence, as a vacuum invites implosion. Their credo is expressed by the narrator of *The Floating Opera*: "Develop, if you can, the technique of the pallbearers and myself: smile, to be sure, but walk on and say nothing." It is Barth's unique talent to catch the gray overcast of such a mind, throwing its aberrations into relief and presenting us with a multiple exposure of its dimensions, in some of the wittiest and most corrosively ironic pages of contemporary American fiction. And some of the most gripping: Barth has the kind of narrative power that can suck a reader into alien worlds almost against his will. Moreover Barth is a writer who is serious about ideas, which is to say that if he is comic he is also disturbing. Amid all the extravagance, a reader must sometimes have the eerie feeling that he is meeting himself in these pages. The books, as Barth suggests, are as much about innocence as nihilism— "the sort of ingenuous fancy that reimagines history and creation, sees the arbitrariness of the universe but shies from its finality." And, he adds, "I'm told this is an American characteristic." And indeed it is.

Born and reared in Maryland, Barth now lives in Pennsylvania with his wife and three children and teaches English at Penn State. At thirty-two he is working on his fourth novel, having to do with "a young boy raised as a goat, as fairy princes were once raised as toads and swans." It will differ from his previous novels, Barth thinks, in that it will deal with "understanding rather than innocence"—but the ingenuous fancy will surely be there. For "a book," says John Barth, "ought to be beautiful—and astonishing."

RICHARD W. MURPHY

37

On Screen: CLAUDIA CARDINALE

Precisely at noon, a young lady in tan touched with crimson stepped into the Antico Caffè Greco in Rome, paused for an effective instant to look six inches above the heads of the coffee drinkers, and then moved with swan's-neck grace to the small marble table in the mirrored corner of the rendezvous room on the Via Condotti. Against this reflected mauresque setting she sat demurely, her face framed by a red straw picture hat, her voice surprisingly husky coming from such an innocent visage; but after a few moments, her languor cracked, revealing through plum-skinned lips the most evenly matched, flashing teeth imaginable. She looked like the well-brought-up granddaughter of an odalisque.

At twenty-three Claudia Cardinale is the most sought-after young actress in European films: Signorina to the Cinecittà-on-the-Tiber directors, Mademoiselle to the Nouvelle Vague-on-the-Seine, and CC (the uncrowned successor to BB? ask the movie magazines) to British and American art film audiences. She is more than another sex symbol; she sums up the new international, coproduction look of the uncommon market for films. It is there in her background: an Italian born in Tunis, whose grandfather came from Sicily, who made her reputation as a cover girl for *Paris-Match* and *L'Europeo* after winning a beauty contest in North Africa, and who speaks English with an ever-so-slight South Carolina (U.S.A.) accent, this last lagniappe from her American secretary.

The silver screen's magic wand tapped her six years ago, when she won the title of Miss Italy of Tunis. Movie offers followed, which she refused for half a year because they seemed so illusory. "I have the head very cold," she explained. Finally, when a role in *Big Deal on Madonna Street* (1959) with Vittorio Gassman came up, she accepted it. She is under contract to Franco Cristaldi of Vides Films, a young producer of this relatively small company, who loans Miss Cardinale's acting services to major film makers on terms that both consider highly satisfactory.

In some twenty films Miss Cardinale has impressed both colleagues and movie-goers; she displayed a common-human touch in addition to her physical attributes (37-23-37). Her attainable—rather than merely lush or symbolic—look came through in *Rocco and His Brothers, Bell' Antonio*, and in *The Girl With the Suitcase*, which she considers her best role. "I never made sexy things in my films," Miss Cardinale insists, pointing out that it would be more accurate for her to be described as a dramatic actress. "It is so stupid all this sex talk. When I am in Paris making *Cartouche* with Jean-Paul Belmondo, everybody treated me like a boy."

This unlikely attitude did not trouble one of her recent Italian directors, who insisted that she be force-fed large quantities of pasta to heighten her looks, for cinema's sake and for *pizzicotto* ("that means pinching"). Nor did it prevent Alberto Moravia—who is so struck by Miss Cardinale that he has written a book about her—from declaring that her beauty comes "from the very strong contrast between the small size of your head and the large size of your body." Miss Cardinale recalls that the novelist asked her some rather odd questions, requesting self-descriptions of the shape of her shoulders and the size of her ear lobes.

Her latest screen roles establish Claudia Cardinale's immediately recognizable international qualities, ear lobes and all, for more than the foreign-language film audiences. Besides *Fellini-8½*, she is cast for a leading part in *The Furnished Room* in Britain and, perhaps more important, she plays the part of Angelica, who marries Burt Lancaster's nephew, in the Titanus–20th-Century-Fox film *The Leopard*. Prince Lampedusa's description of Angelica, the lovely and ambitious daughter of the rising middle class, seemed to suit Claudia: "She was tall and well made, on an ample scale; her skin looked as if it had the flavor of fresh cream, which it resembled; her childlike mouth, that of strawberries. . . . She was moving slowly, making her wide white skirt rotate around her, and emanating from her whole person was the invincible calm of a woman sure of her beauty. Only many months later was it known that at the moment of that victorious entry she had been on the point of fainting from anxiety."

Miss Cardinale sipped her cappuccino, twisted her carried gloves, twice powdered her nose, and finally asked, "Do you like my hat?" Reassured, she explained that she had never worn a picture hat before and, "I am a little embarrassed." Something of that same wide-eyed innocence and wonder at herself had become evident some months before at a command performance before the Queen of England. Representing Italian artists at the behest of President Gronchi, she stood near Dany Robin of France, Melina Mercouri of Greece, Peter Sellers of Britain. When she removed her pink cape, revealing a daringly low-cut gown, there was an explosion of flesh and gasps. It was a sight fit for a king or, at the least, Anthony Armstrong-Jones. Queen Elizabeth came up to her and asked, "Are you in England making a film?" Miss Cardinale replied, "No, Your Majesty, I'm here only to see you."

As she rose to leave the Antico Caffè Greco, a callipygian vision, she caused heads to turn in any language: CC was not merely an Italian, not merely French, but that mixture of south wind and burnished sun, a Mediterranean.

HERBERT MITGANG

38

TWENTY-FIVE CENTURIES OF

PERSIA

Besieged through history by Greeks, Romans, Arabs, Turks, and Mongols, the throne of Cyrus still stands. From it ninety kings have given their patronage to a brilliant cultural tradition

By TERENCE O'DONNELL

40

The tomb of Cyrus the Great, founder of the Persian Empire, still stands in his capital, Pasargadae, or "the camp of the Persians." If, as some ancient sources say, the King once rested in a golden sarcophagus, both he and it are long since gone. His inscription read: "Here I lie, Cyrus, King of Kings."

Sometime this year, at the ruins of the palace of Persepolis, it is planned to celebrate the 2,500th anniversary of the oldest political institution on earth—the Persian monarchy.* The first King of Kings, as the Persian monarchs have usually styled themselves, was Cyrus the Great, born in the sixth century B.C. The present and roughly ninetieth king of Persia is His Imperial Majesty, Mohammed Reza Pahlavi. Between these two men lies a history of political survival and cultural endurance that has not been matched by any other nation.

Time and again the thread of Persian history has been severed by violence and lost in foreign invasion. For this barren plateau, uninviting though it seems, is the land bridge between three continents, and so has drawn down upon itself the fiercest races and the most ambitious princes of all the surrounding lands. From the wild and windy plains to the north came the Parthians, the Turks, and the bloodthirsty Mongols. From the burning deserts to the south came the hard-riding, God-inflamed Arabs. From the west came the disciplined legions of Greece and Rome. It was Persia's genius to absorb and mold them all. Her dynasties might be overthrown, her palaces burned, her cities heaped with skulls. But the native spirit survived to raise new cities and crown new kings and to impress upon her conquerors the stamp of a civilization that remained essentially Persian.

More than that of other nations, Persia's history is a history of her monarchs. Under their rule, benevolent or harsh, the nation swept to every victory, and around their enduring memory it rallied after every defeat. In culture, as in politics, their influence was crucial. All the characteristic arts—the gold- and silverwork, the poetry and painting, the rugs and tiles and palace architecture—owe their existence to royal patronage, and some of the bloodiest tyrants were the most discriminating connoisseurs. In the beginning these kings were tribal chieftains, no different in origin or status from the kings of Sumer and Babylon and Assyria who ruled the neighboring lands before them. But they raised kingship to a high art and set a universal pattern of imperial rule.

It was early in the first millennium B.C., somewhere beyond the Black and Caspian seas, that the tribes we know as Persians began to move. Why they were moving is not certain. Perhaps their flocks had increased beyond the available pasturage, perhaps drought had come, perhaps they were being pushed. At any rate, down they rode, leather-helmeted, their horses slung with bronze ornaments, to the plateau that lay between their own Eurasian steppes and the civilized world of Western Asia. They tried to cross over. They were stopped, at least for a time. Here then they settled down, on the plateau since called Iran; that is, "the land of the Aryans."

To us, nearly three thousand years later, "Iran" seems a modern name, something thought up after oil was discovered, and we wonder why the plateau isn't called by its "old" name, Persia. Yet to the Iranians the plateau has never been known by that name. Only a part of it in the far south was called Pars, the Greek Persis, the English Persia; and the tribe who lived there, the Persians, were only one of the Iranian tribes to come down from the north. Still, for us, the name Persia has associations that Iran does not, and since a name should ring, we prefer to persist in our old mistake.

Among the other tribesmen who came from the steppes were the Medes who lived northwest of the Persians near the present Iraqi border. These two tribes developed more or less separately until the sixth century B.C.; then, with a king and his dream, their joint history began. Herodotus tells us

---

* In such an ancient chronology the dating of the year 1 is bound to be somewhat arbitrary. In planning the official celebration (perhaps this year, perhaps next), the Persian government is concerned not only by dynastic history but also by such matters as international politics and the availability of tourist hotels.

Mohammed Reza Pahlavi, the present King of Kings, here seen outside his palace in Teheran, is the second monarch of the Pahlavi line. His father was an army colonel who seized the throne in 1925. The Pahlavis have largely rid Persia of foreign influence and have begun the ambitious task of modernization.

that Astyages, king of the Medes, gave his daughter, Mandane, in marriage to Cambyses, a Persian of the Achaemenid clan. Before the birth of Cyrus, their son, Mandane's father dreamed that from his daughter's womb a vine would grow, covering all of Asia. The dream was prophetic.

First Cyrus united the Iranians by conquering the Medes, and from the Medes, to whom it had fallen some years before, he gained most of Assyria. Then with the Medes he went on to take Lydia and the Greek city states of Asia Minor, the eastern kingdoms that lay in the region of the Oxus and Jaxartes rivers, and finally, nearer to home, the Babylonian empire, which fell to him in 539 B.C. The vine rooted in Pars (the modern Fars) had in eleven years spread west to the Mediterranean and east to India; the Persian Empire, the largest the world had known, was founded.

More significant than its size is the manner in which the Empire was governed. The administrative system, created mainly by Darius, the third Achaemenid to reign, was headed by the king himself who, with the aid of a council of nobles and a court of law, ruled with absolute power an empire divided into twenty provinces. Each province was administered by a satrap, with the help of an independent general and a royal secretary, all three of whom were reported on by traveling officials called "the eyes and ears of the king." To promote the economic well-being of his empire, Darius instituted an orderly tax system, uniform coinage, standard weights and measures. He built irrigation systems in Central Asia and the Syrian Desert, harbors on the Persian Gulf, a canal from the Nile to Suez, and a road system—the first ever built for wheeled vehicles—on which relays of horsemen could carry a message over sixteen hundred miles, from Susa to Sardis, in a week. Finally, with less arrogance than most imperial rulers, the Achaemenids chose for the Empire's lingua franca not their own Persian but the more

widely spoken Aramaic. The early Achaemenid administration of the Persian state formed a primer that later governments read with care.

The greatness of the Empire lay not only in the order, material welfare, and peace that it conferred but more especially in its basic humanity. Cyrus, for example, left intact many a captured capital and more than once returned to positions of honor rulers whom he had earlier deposed. Even the Greek city states of Asia Minor were allowed to keep their constitutions. More surprisingly, especially when we reflect on the history of the Christian West, the conquered nations were encouraged to keep their own religions. When Cyrus entered Babylon, he ordered that all the idols seized by the Babylonians as trophies from other nations be restored to their native temples. The Jews, released from their Babylonian captivity, were permitted to return to Jerusalem where, with funds from their own treasury, Cyrus and Darius had their temple rebuilt.

There was, of course, as in all things Persian, some craft in all of this—the silk glove on the iron fist. Yet not entirely iron, for there was in the Persian make-up an alloy, their religion—a religion, to quote Renan, that was "the least pagan in the pagan world."

Zoroaster, contemporary with the first Achaemenids, preached that there are two forces in the universe: good and evil. Good is embodied in Ahura Mazda, evil in Ahriman. Man, by adhering to Zoroaster's ethical triad of good thoughts, good words, and good deeds, joins with Ahura Mazda in the defeat of evil and thereby gains immortality. One God instead of many, a God of justice and beneficence rather than a God of vengeance, a moral code for this world, judgment and immortality in the next—these were some of the concepts that enlightened Persian rule and that, joined with Persian administrative skill, made the Empire great.

Persian architecture reflected Persian religion and the Persian state. There were no temples; Zoroastrianism was too abstract a religion, too devoid of idol and rite, to produce anything more than open-air altars and small stone towers for the sacred fire. But there were palaces and they were magnificent, for the Persian political system glorified the monarch as the embodiment of all power and all wisdom, and therefore the artistic resources of all the Empire were concentrated on his house.

The first and perhaps most simple of these palaces was built by Cyrus at Pasargadae, in the form of a group of pavilions scattered through a park. In some of these pavilions there were high, white-walled rooms, their doorways and alcoves rimmed with black, the shafts of the columns white between black bases and capitals. At Susa, built mainly by Darius, the buildings were grouped around open courts, their floors surfaced with polished red ochre, the walls—as at Pasargadae—white but here inlaid with panels of glazed brick representing heraldic animals and royal guards.

The greatest of the Achaemenid centers, however, was Persepolis, built by Darius and his successors in Pars (see pages 46–47). Here, facing a broad plain, at the foot of the Mountain of Mercy, the builders clamped together great blocks of stone to form a terrace fifteen hundred feet long and nine hundred wide. Branching stairways set into the façade of the terrace—stairways broad enough to accommodate ten horsemen riding abreast—led to the vast platform. Here stood the palaces, their fluted stone pillars, the highest in the ancient world, rising to roofs of cedar inlaid with precious metals.

Much, of course, was borrowed. After all the Persians were a new people, having brought from the steppes little more than their horses, some ornaments, physical vigor, and clear intellects. Moreover, they ruled an empire—Egypt, Macedonia, and parts of Greece had been added by Cyrus's immediate successors—and they wished to reflect the extent and richness of this realm in their architecture. Still, the result was not eclectic but Persian, for in these palaces the kings sought to echo, in the richest of materials and on a lordly scale, the old wooden halls of their ancestors. The stone pillars, for example—brought from Elam, cut by Ionians, embellished perhaps by Egyptians—tapered away at the top like the tree-trunk pillars that supported those halls. The terrace, the very foundation of the palace complex, was not, as in Mesopotamia, a defense against armies and flood but rather a means of display, a kind of gigantic dais on which to mount the power and pomp of the Persian throne.

Today the remains of Persepolis lie strewn as though a sea had passed over the place, yet enough is left to make it one of the loveliest ruins on earth. There are the pillars, a dozen or so out of the hundreds that once rose from the terrace, some with bell-shaped bases petaled with lotus leaves. There are doorways with flared lintels of great beauty and a gateway showing, in bas-relief, Darius himself beneath a tasseled canopy, looking like a Greek priest with his bun of hair and high round hat. Finally, there is the best of Persepolis, now and probably then, the sculptured stairways of the Apadana.

The Apadana was an audience hall where, at the vernal equinox, the Persian New Year, representatives from the Empire came to the king with gifts—just as today on March 21, in Teheran at the Gulistan palace, the grandest levee of the year takes place. At the Apadana this procession was reproduced in bas-reliefs that panel the eastern stairway and platform walls. On one side, in three registers, there are lines of attendants and courtiers. The attendants, led by an usher, walk with folded rugs tucked under their arms, one with the royal footstool strapped to his back. These are followed by a trio of grooms, their arms flung over the backs of the royal horses—three little pacers with plumes. At the end come the king's chariots. Below walk the courtiers with big rings in their left ears, the Persians wearing fluted tiaras and long

TEXT CONTINUED ON PAGE 49

THE ROYAL RESIDENCE OF PERSEPOLIS

The great King of Kings, Xerxes, protected by the royal umbrella, still seems to be overseeing the construction of the royal compound begun by his father, Darius I, in 521 B.C. This weathered stone relief on the eastern doorway stands among the vast ruins of the Achaemenid palace.

OVERLEAF: *At the foot of the Mountain of Mercy architects, probably from Egypt, first had to shape over a million square feet of rocky slope. In this northern air view of the terrace, the pillars of the Apadana, or audience hall (left, background), dominate the plain. The Gate of Xerxes (see page 48) stands behind, and the palace of Darius in front. The large cluster to the right (background) of the Apadana is the Hall of the Hundred Columns, in which the royal treasures were exhibited. The harem of Xerxes, now restored, stands before it (foreground). It was to this seat of Persian power that Alexander the Great put the torch in 331 B.C. Evidence of violent conflagration has been found in the excavations of the Apadana and treasury areas.*

robes hiked at the waist, the Medes wearing dome-shaped hats, and jackets and trousers. Some of the courtiers step gravely forward holding flowers while others fuss and shuffle, turning back to chat or holding hands.

On the other side of the staircase walk the emissaries from the Empire: Scythians in high pointed hoods, long-robed Arabians, Syrians wearing curious horn-shaped turbans—more than twenty nations are represented. In groups of half a dozen or so, divided by stylized cypress trees, the embassies hold aloft their gifts for the king. There are heavy torques and bracelets, bows and long daggers, urns and ointment jars. The Cilicians come with cloth and two fine rams. The Indians lead a donkey, and the Ethiopians, a giraffe. There are camels from Arabia, from Susa, a lioness and two cubs. Stallions, apparently the most prized gift, come from Cappadocia, Armenia, and Scythia. In slow processional these figures move toward the audience hall to show the diversity and the allegiance of the peoples over whom the King of Kings extends his rule.

The reliefs have a decorative quality beyond mere representation. In part it is expressed through the grouping, stance, and gesture of human and animal figures. More especially it lies in details: the rosette, the cypress tree, and the lotus; those tight little clusters of whorled stone that make up the curls of beard and hair; an animal leash looped with the grace of an arabesque; the splay of lines in a drape set off by folds of bare stone. This decorative element, already so pronounced at Persepolis, was later to become, with the help of the Islamic prohibition against representation, the prime characteristic of all Persian art.

Persepolis, seat and symbol of the Empire, lasted no more than a century and a half after the time of Darius. There was in the first place an inherent precariousness in the imperial system, the centrifugal forces of diversity threatening cohesion. Secondly, there was internal decline. Many of the later kings were harem-bred fops whose administration was both inefficient and cruel; among the Persians themselves bribery began to replace bravery as more and more in the field they depended upon foreign mercenaries. Yet it was neither inherent weakness nor internal decline that in itself ended the Empire. (Even in the later period there were kings of ability and times of reform, and there would have been

others had the Empire continued.) Rather it was a shock from the outside, perhaps the strongest shock the world had known: Alexander the Great. In 331 B.C. he defeated the Persians and burned Persepolis.*

It had been a great beginning. In less than a hundred years —from Cyrus the Great to Darius the Great—these Aryan Persians from the steppes had produced a religion, the first with Judaism to replace blood rites and idols with one God and a moral system; a government, the first to go so far in realizing what has always been the basic need in the political world, a diversity of nations living in peace and under one just rule; and finally an art, not only great in itself but the precursor of a decorative genius that was to create some of the most beautiful designs in the world.

Two centuries of Greek rule made little difference. That the Persians, the most imitative of people, should have remained indifferent to the Greek example, one of the most potent in history, is extraordinary. The reason may lie in the fact that the Persians and Greeks were more than simply different. They were opposites, as opposite in political life as the city state and the absolute monarchy, in art as representation and decoration. In this case, at any rate, East and West did not meet.

The Persian protest first became effective in the middle of the second century B.C., when the Parthians, an Iranian tribe from the north, revolted against the Greek Seleucids and established their own empire. The Parthians were in turn succeeded in A.D. 226 by the Sasanians who, coming from the old homeland of Pars and claiming descent from the Achaemenids, repudiated even more thoroughly the lingering influence of the Greeks. With the Sasanians the Persian ethos in government, religion, and art was re-established, to last until the Arab invasions of the seventh century and even beyond.

As he was dying, Alexander ordered that Persia be divided among ninety princes. Certainly for some centuries, before the time of the Sasanians, the country was seldom much more than an assortment of fractious, petty states. The Sasanians re-created a centralized monarchy with a legal and administrative system equaling that of the Achaemenids and a military machine which once again brought the Persians to the Nile and the Mediterranean. Here they clashed first

* See "The Two Worlds of Alexander" by C. A. Robinson, Jr., for March, 1959.

Past the winged man-bull on the Gate of Xerxes at Persepolis, came the nations of the Empire seeking the King's justice. The portal is inscribed in Persian, Elamite, and Babylonian: "I [am] Xerxes the great king, king of kings, king of the countries possessing many kinds of people, king of this great earth far and wide, the son of Darius the king, the Achaemenid. Says Xerxes the great king: By the grace of Ahura Mazda, this gateway of all lands I made; much else [that is] beautiful [was] done throughout Parsa which I did and which my father did; whatever work seems beautiful, all that we did by the grace of Ahura Mazda."

with Rome, then with Byzantium, as their predecessors had clashed with the Greeks. The Romans were often humbled, the emperor Valerian himself being brought back captive to Pars (see opposite); yet the Persians did not succeed in conquering the world from the Romans but only in sharing it.

We hear something of the personal style of the Persians of this period from a Roman named Ammianus Marcellinus. He tells us that they were a slender, rather dark people with an easy gait and that they kept their beards like dandies, loved bangles and above all pearls. Highly superstitious, they never ate fruit in foreign places for fear of poison or spells. They were also talkative and a little boastful. As soldiers they were not so much dashing as crafty. In love, the earnest Roman concludes, they indulged to excess. It is a description that in some respects fits today as well as then, and that the Persians, more ready than most people to admit their faults, would probably accept, balking only when Marcellinus accuses them of having "goatlike" eyes. Vain of their beauty, proud especially of their eyes, they would remind us that Marcellinus was a knobby-kneed Roman and judge him envious.

The court at which these foppish but tough little grandees

PERSIA AGAINST THE WEST

Persia's long struggle with the West was fought first with the Greeks and then with the Romans. In 499 B.C. the revolt of the Greek cities on the west coast of Asia Minor touched off a long contest filled with heroic defenses (Marathon in 490 B.C.) and sackings of cities (Athens in 480–479 B.C.), as well as hand-to-hand combats like that shown on this contemporary Greek plate (at top). This seesaw struggle was ended decisively by Alexander, shown above on a sarcophagus from Sidon as he routs the Persians at the Battle of Issus in 333 B.C. Four hundred years later the Romans began a long campaign to conquer Persia, only to suffer a bitter defeat with the capture of the emperor Valerian by the Sasanian king Shapur I in A.D. 260. The surrender of Valerian, the only Western Roman emperor who ever fell into enemy hands, is immortalized (opposite) in the rock cliffs of Naqsh-i-Rustam near Persepolis. Legend says Shapur kept the old man alive to use as a steppingstone when mounting his horse.

gathered was located at Ctesiphon, near the present Baghdad, in a building that was significantly different from the Achaemenid palaces. The dome and vault replaced the column and flat roof: these two forms, together with the older *talar,* the pillared porch or hall, were to characterize Persian architecture throughout the rest of its history. The audience hall at Ctesiphon was one hundred twenty-one feet high and was roofed with a vault spanning eighty-four feet. In winter the floor was laid with "The Spring of Khosrau," the first Persian carpet of which we know, ninety feet square, woven of silk and embellished with gold and silver thread to represent a garden in spring. The carpet glittered with jewels by the hundred thousand: diamonds for water courses, emeralds for greenery, rubies and other precious stones for plumage and blossoms. At the end of the vast hall, beyond transparent curtains, sat the king on a golden throne, stiffened ribbons of gold flowing up from his shoulders, and his crown, because of its great weight and size, suspended above him.

From the *Shah Nameh,* the Persian national epic, we know a great deal about these Sasanian kings. Shapur I was not only a warrior—it was he who captured the emperor Valerian—but a scholar responsible for the translation of many Greek and Latin classics. It was he also who continued the Persian tradition of religious tolerance and proclaimed, according to an Armenian source, that "Magi, Manichaean, Jew, Christian, and all men of whatever religion should be left undisturbed and at peace." Khosrau I showed a like devotion to learning and tolerance. It was at his court that the seven Greek philosophers, driven from Byzantium, were given refuge and stipends. And it was he who, ascending the throne as a young man, said: "We find no fear or lack which sticketh harder at a man than that he should be without a good king," a statement which gives credence to the legend that the bell he placed outside his palace for those who had complaints went untouched for seven years. The same Khosrau is credited with introducing from India the royal game of chess. Polo, that other royal game, may have originated in the northern steppes but was developed in Persia, and after hunting and hawking was the principal sport of the Sasanian kings. Music, too, was greatly valued, for we read in the *Shah Nameh* that Bahram I, hearing that the poor complained of having to dance without accompaniment, imported ten thousand gypsy musicians into the country.

Silk, silver, and stone were the favorite materials of Sasa-

PERSIAN RULERS				EVENTS
Achaemenids	550			
		490	Battle of Marathon	
		331	Alexander burns Persepolis	
Seleucids; Parthians	312			
		190	Romans defeat Seleucids at Magnesia	
B.C.		92	Rome-Parthia treaty	B.C.
A.D.				A.D.
Sasanians	226			
		260	Emperor Valerian captured	
		476	Fall of Rome	
Early Islamic	c.650			
		800	Charlemagne's coronation	
Seljuks	1040			
		1096	First Crusade	
Mongols; Il-Kahns	c.1220			
		1271	Marco Polo reaches Persia	
Tamerlane; Timurids	c.1385			
		1453	Fall of Constantinople	
Safavids	1502			
		1601	English open sea trade with Persia	
		1724	Russia and Turkey seize Persian territory	
Afsharids, Zands, Qajars	1736			
		1800	Napoleon seeks Persian alliance	
Pahlavis	1925			

nian artists. From Parthian times the great Silk Road from China had passed through Persia on its way to the West. Royal patronage and the nation's love of luxury now combined to produce a golden age of silk design. So widespread was the fame of their precious fabrics that today in certain Western churches the bones of early Christian saints are wrapped in shrouds of Sasanian silk.

In stone the exaltation of the king was the principal aim of the Sasanian artists. Much of their work is near Persepolis, carved into the stone cliffs of Naqsh-i-Rustum, and farther south at a place called Shapur. Here, above the green banks of a shallow, spreading river, they hacked out in the yellow rock of the valley walls great rectangular tableaux of playing-card kings, heraldic figures posed in the triumph of war or the glory of the chase. These figures are entirely different from those at Persepolis. There somewhat less than life-sized figures, chiseled and clean on their panels of stone, proceed with the mandarin calm of a settled power. The Sasanians, on the other hand, never defeated but never permanently winning, were warriors more than rulers and thus on the stone cliffs we have an art that is massive and boastful.

The Sasanian dynasty produced its share of tyrants and the Empire suffered periods of oppression and chaos. Yet the culture created by the Sasanian kings was a balanced and brilliant achievement. Though soldiers, off to the wars or the hunt half their lives, they were nonetheless capable of enjoying in their leisure the refinements of civilized life. Shapur I was one of the early protectors of Mani, founder of the native Persian faith Manichaeism, which in time was to spread west as far as France and even threaten Rome. Another Persian religion, the Mazdakite movement, was at the time of its inception championed by Kavadh I. Nestorianism, the Christian sect in Persia, received the protection and in some cases the encouragement of several Sasanian monarchs. Meanwhile, by their patronage they created in the stoutly vaulted palace halls, in the great stone tableaux, and in splendid silks, silver, plates, and bronze vessels, a vigorous and handsome art whose influence affected both China and medieval Europe. Since the time of Cyrus, a thousand years of Persian history had passed. The Sasanian achievement was a fitting millenary.

Throughout these thousand years the Persians, although invaded from many quarters, had had nothing to fear from that desert peninsula which lay so near them across the Persian Gulf. Here lived a scattered, nomadic people possessed of little more than sheep and a waste on which to graze them. In the early seventh century, however, these lizard-eaters, as the Persians called the Arabs, were inspired by the creed of Mohammed. United now by a common faith and filled with missionary spirit, they moved out in all directions from the peninsula and conquered in the name of Allah. In Persia, as elsewhere in the East, they encountered little resistance, and by 642 most of Persia was annexed to the Arab Empire.

With the Arab occupation Persian history would appear to break in half. As we divide our history with Christ, so it is customary, when speaking of Persia, to refer to the Islamic and pre-Islamic periods. Literature, art, and architecture, as well as religion, were affected; yet the root of the Persian ethos was never touched and it continued to determine the basic nature of Persian culture in all its manifestations. In art the Islamic prohibition against portrayal of the human form simply reinforced the Persian proclivity for decoration. In literature, though the Persians borrowed its alphabet and many words from Arabic, it was Persian, not Arabic, that became the language of diplomats and poets from India to Turkey. Finally, and most importantly, in the sphere of religion the Persians developed a faith as distinct from orthodox Islam as Protestantism is from Catholicism, or in terms more local, as the settled Aryan Persian from the nomadic Arab Semite. "After all," as the historian of Persian literature Edward Browne has said, "the change was but skin deep."

Arab political dominion was even less substantial. A hundred years after the invasion Persian bureaucrats were in virtual control of their own administration, and less than a century after this in Khurasan, the first Persian principality was granted autonomy. This breakaway continued until the tenth century, when the Persians once again ruled their own house. It was, however, a divided rule for, as after the Greek invasion, the country was simply an assemblage of petty states.

These internal divisions hardly made for peace, but they did encourage the arts. Each of the little courts strove to get its share of scholars and artists who, presented with such a variety of patronage, were free to choose those courts most congenial to their pursuits. In the east the Samanid kings lured to their capital at Bokhara scholars like Avicenna, who served as the royal physician; here also lived Rudaki and Dakiki, the earliest Persian poets. In the south the kings of the Buyid dynasty built magnificently appointed libraries and kept encyclopedists busy recording all the knowledge of the day. Up among the forests of the Caspian coast the Ziyarids produced, in a tower and a book (see page 60), two impressive memorials to the period.

For about a hundred years these dynasties continued to rule Persia, bringing back all the old Persian loves: learning and art, palaces and gardens, ceremony and elegance. Then, once again, the country was invaded, this time by the Seljuk Turks and Mongols of Central Asia.

Persia's history is the history of invasions. On those occasions when they have been united and strong under the leadership of an able king, the Persians threw the interlopers out. More often, as nations frequently invaded are prone to do, they collaborated. Thus it is that in the thirteen hundred years since the fall of the Sasanians the Persians have been political masters in their own house for little more than four centuries.

How, then, were they able during these long periods of political domination to preserve their culture? Why, like the Byzantines, did they not become Turks? In the first place the Persians were good administrators whereas the invaders were mainly nomads who knew nothing of that art. Thus throughout almost all the occupations administration remained in Persian hands. Secondly, the Persians were seldom invaded by a people more civilized than they, and so they were often tutors as well as civil servants to their foreign rulers. Said an Arab caliph: "The Persians ruled for a thousand years and did not need us even for a day; we have been ruling for one or two centuries, and cannot do without them for an hour."

The Turks and Mongols are a case in point. They ruled through such great Persian viziers as Nizam-ul-Mulk and Rashid-ud-Din, and under their tutelage they became devotees and patrons of the Persian arts. It is not, therefore, surprising that during this four-hundred-year occupation—the longest the Persians have known—Persian culture prevailed. Indeed, it flourished, for it was during this time that architecture, literature, and painting reached their greatest height.

Architecture before Islam was to be found mainly in pal-

TEXT CONTINUED ON PAGE 57

THE ROYAL ARTISTS

"Nations long steeped in luxury," was Alexander's scornful description of the foe. Indeed, even before they reached the royal capitals, the Macedonians were amazed at the Persians' opulence on the battlefield—from the embroidered tapestries hung in the royal tents to the cups, armlets, and collars of gold taken from fallen soldiers. The Achaemenid artists who so adorned their warriors were in the king's employ, working as skillfully in silver from Egypt as in gold from Lydia and Bactria. The following pages show two of the finest examples of Achaemenid craftsmanship. The gold rhyton, or drinking vessel (overleaf, left), in the form of a winged lion, 6th–5th century B.C., is thought to come from Hamadan, the ancient Ecbatana, site of the royal treasury and summer residence of the Persian kings. The lotus buds and arches on the rim resemble Assyrian motifs. The graceful silver ibex (overleaf, right), 6th–4th century B.C., inlaid in gold, is one of a pair of handles which probably adorned a nobleman's vase.
OVERLEAF: LEFT, ARCHAEOLOGICAL MUSEUM, TEHERAN; RIGHT, LOUVRE

Most of Persia's great art has been devoted to the exaltation of kings. The antlered monarch at right belongs to the Sasanian dynasty, which revived Persian power and Persian culture in the third century A.D. *The greatest of these monarchs is depicted in the center of the Cup of Khosrau I, opposite. Rimmed in gold, the cup has three concentric circles of carved crystal and brightly colored glass inlays.*

TEXT CONTINUED FROM PAGE 53

aces. After the fall of the Sasanians the palace, like the institution it represented, became smaller and less significant. With Islam the mosque took its place as the primary end of architectural effort. A mosque was in many ways like a medieval cathedral. It was a place of prayer and a place of refuge, a school, a court of justice, and a meeting place. In appearance, however, it differed in two startling ways from the cathedral, for it often had no façade and the courts were open to the sky.

In early Islam public prayer took place in any open space large enough to accommodate the congregation; that is, a square. In time, with the desire to enclose, to protect and beautify, the square was walled to become a court. Thus, except for its arcaded sides and the domed sanctuary at its end, the mosque was without a roof. And, except for the portal, it often had no visible exterior walls, for the important surfaces were all within the court. One important characteristic of mosque architecture and of much other Persian architecture is that it is interior and private.

As the basic structure was elaborated, the mosque displayed four characteristic forms: a large and elaborate portal arch; great vaulted recesses, called *ivans,* in each of the walls surrounding the court; the paired minarets flanking the great dome; and beneath the dome, the sanctuary, which contains the *mihrab,* an arched panel marking the direction of Mecca, toward which the faithful pray.

By the end of the Seljuk period, in the thirteenth century, most of these forms were fully developed, and what we think of as the Persian mosque was completed—except perhaps for the most familiar aspects of the tiled interiors and domes. Since Achaemenid times, various kinds of faïence decoration had been used in Persian architecture. However, with the development of the technique of faïence mosaic—segments of different-colored tiles set in a design on a plaster bed—it became possible to face the entire surface of a building with brilliant color. Decoration of this sort required that a building have substantial mass and strong and simple forms, for otherwise its architectural qualities would be overwhelmed by the decoration. Under the Timurids, in the fifteenth century, the architect and decorator brought these factors of mass and form and decoration into balance and so produced in its most perfect form the Persian mosque.

To properly appreciate a mosque one must remember two things. The first is that it is a mosque and not a church. If, when we enter it, we have the idea at the back of our minds, as many of us do, that the house of God is a shadowed place, then we may feel that in these sun-filled courts banked with glittering color there is something discordant and wrong. There is nothing wrong; there is only much that is different. Then, coming from the verdant West, where such color displays would seem gaudy, it is difficult for us to see the mosque as the man from the desert does, or the man who has lived his life in the baked clay lanes of a Persian town. To these men it means much to rest by the pool and gaze at the screens of sapphire tile, at the great dome with its whirling arabesques, for they are parched in more than one sense and, as their thirst is quenched by the water of the pool, so their eyes drink in the colors of the mosque and are refreshed.

Nothing could be more different from the mosque than that other form which flourished during the Timurid period, the miniature (see pages 61–66). A mosque is massive, spectacular, and public. Miniatures are aristocratic and delicate. They were meant to go with wine and ease and to offer delight by their subtle effects. Miniatures may have had their

TEXT CONTINUED ON PAGE 67

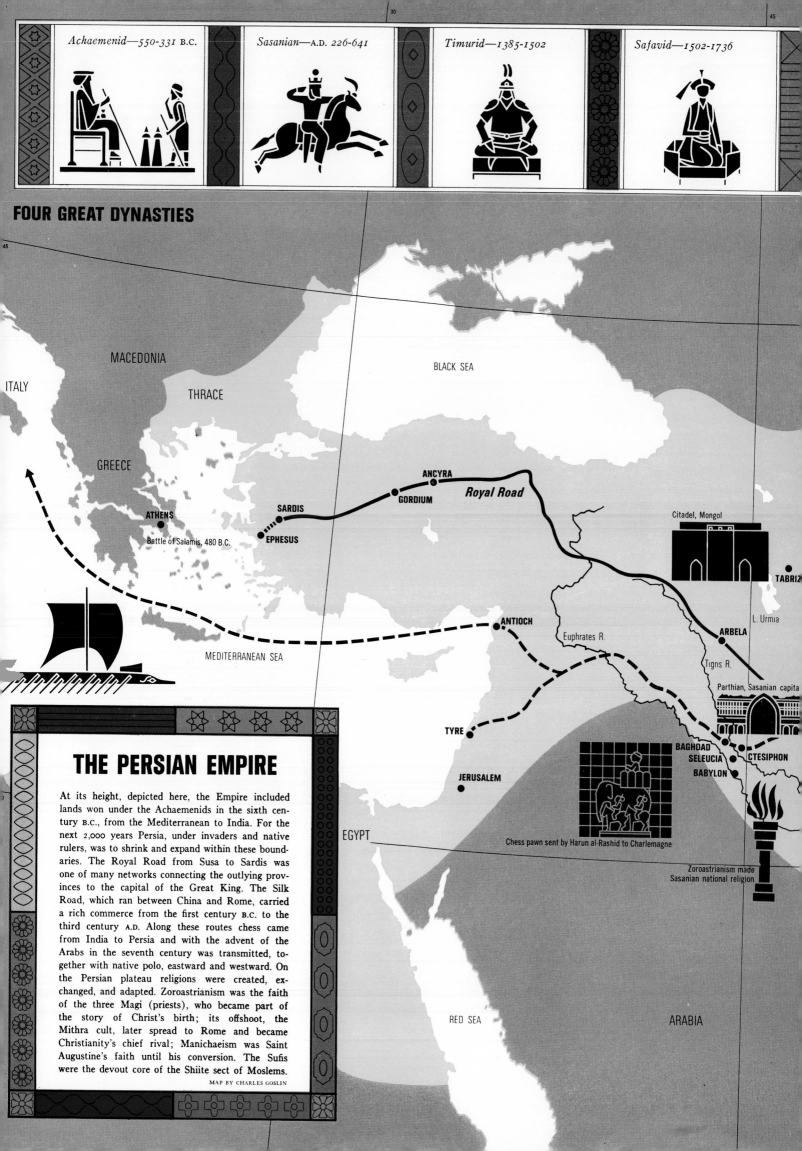

Achaemenid—550-331 B.C. *Sasanian—A.D. 226-641* *Timurid—1385-1502* *Safavid—1502-1736*

FOUR GREAT DYNASTIES

MACEDONIA

BLACK SEA

ITALY

THRACE

GREECE

ATHENS

Battle of Salamis, 480 B.C.

SARDIS

EPHESUS

GORDIUM

ANCYRA

Royal Road

Citadel, Mongol

TABRIZ

L. Urmia

ANTIOCH

Euphrates R.

ARBELA

Tigris R.

Parthian, Sasanian capital

MEDITERRANEAN SEA

TYRE

BAGHDAD

SELEUCIA

CTESIPHON

JERUSALEM

BABYLON

Chess pawn sent by Harun al-Rashid to Charlemagne

EGYPT

Zoroastrianism made
Sasanian national religion

RED SEA

ARABIA

THE PERSIAN EMPIRE

At its height, depicted here, the Empire included lands won under the Achaemenids in the sixth century B.C., from the Mediterranean to India. For the next 2,000 years Persia, under invaders and native rulers, was to shrink and expand within these boundaries. The Royal Road from Susa to Sardis was one of many networks connecting the outlying provinces to the capital of the Great King. The Silk Road, which ran between China and Rome, carried a rich commerce from the first century B.C. to the third century A.D. Along these routes chess came from India to Persia and with the advent of the Arabs in the seventh century was transmitted, together with native polo, eastward and westward. On the Persian plateau religions were created, exchanged, and adapted. Zoroastrianism was the faith of the three Magi (priests), who became part of the story of Christ's birth; its offshoot, the Mithra cult, later spread to Rome and became Christianity's chief rival; Manichaeism was Saint Augustine's faith until his conversion. The Sufis were the devout core of the Shiite sect of Moslems.

MAP BY CHARLES GOSLIN

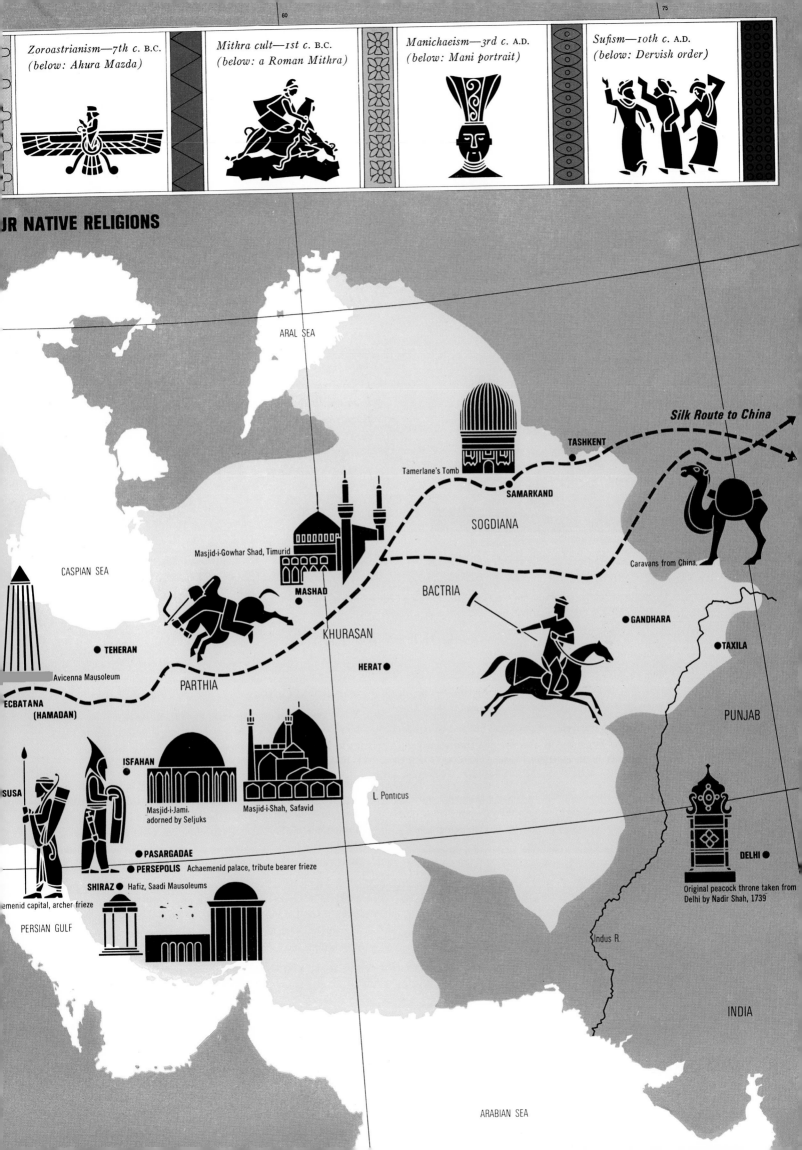

Zoroastrianism—7th c. B.C.
(below: Ahura Mazda)

Mithra cult—1st c. B.C.
(below: a Roman Mithra)

Manichaeism—3rd c. A.D.
(below: Mani portrait)

Sufism—10th c. A.D.
(below: Dervish order)

JR NATIVE RELIGIONS

ARAL SEA

Silk Route to China

TASHKENT

Tamerlane's Tomb

SAMARKAND

SOGDIANA

Masjid-i-Gowhar Shad, Timurid

Caravans from China.

CASPIAN SEA

BACTRIA

MASHAD

GANDHARA

KHURASAN

TAXILA

TEHERAN

Avicenna Mausoleum

HERAT

PARTHIA

PUNJAB

ECBATANA
(HAMADAN)

SUSA

ISFAHAN

L. Ponticus

Masjid-i-Jami,
adorned by Seljuks

Masjid-i-Shah, Safavid

DELHI

PASARGADAE

PERSEPOLIS   Achaemenid palace, tribute bearer frieze

Original peacock throne taken from
Delhi by Nadir Shah, 1739

SHIRAZ   Hafiz, Saadi Mausoleums

emenid capital, archer frieze

Indus R.

PERSIAN GULF

INDIA

ARABIAN SEA

THE INVADERS: ARAB AND MONGOL

Invasion, destruction, and the growth of a new culture based on the Persian style with foreign overlays: such is the recurring pattern in Persia's history. The Ziyarid kings who ruled the southern shores of the Caspian after the Arab conquest of A.D. 650 were men of taste and judgment. One of their monuments is the tomb of Qabus, the poet-king, which overlooks the Turkoman plain, two hundred feet of lemon-yellow brick (left). Legend says that his crystal coffin hung from the conical roof beside a little window that let in the rays of the morning sun. Even the Mongols, who laid Persia waste in the thirteenth century, were wise patrons of the arts. Tamerlane, the classic symbol of bloodlust, appears in the miniature on the opposite page as a fairy-tale prince entering his capital of Samarkand.

A Mirror for Princes

The Ziyarid prince, Kai Kaus, grandson of Qabus, wrote a book of conduct and etiquette called the Qabus Nameh, *for his own son, in 1082. A model of noble manners, it includes these lines:*

"Be of ready speech, my son, yet never tell lies and do not gain the reputation of being a liar. Rather become known for veracity, so that if ever in an emergency you utter a lie it will be believed.

However well informed you may be, behave as though you were less competent than you are in fact, so that when the time comes for speech and action you may not be left standing helpless.

On all occasions rise from your wine while you still have room for two glasses more, and guard yourself against both that last morsel of food which brings over-satiety and the cup which brings drunkenness, for over-satiety and drunkenness are not the results of the sum total that one eats and drinks; but the one comes from the last morsel and the other from the last cup.

If you drink wine, let it be the finest; if you listen to music let it be the sweetest and if you commit a forbidden act, let it be with a beautiful partner, so that even though you may be convicted of sin in the next world, you will at any rate not be branded a fool in this.

When you set out to ride, never mount a horse that is too small; however handsome a man may be, he appears insignificant on a little horse, whereas although a man may be insignificant in stature he appears to great advantage on a big horse.

Once you have married a wife, being greatly in love with her, even though you may be infatuated with her, do not spend every night in her society. Let it be only from time to time, thus leading her to think that such is the universal custom, so that if on occasion you have reason for excusing yourself or wish to go on a journey, your wife will be forbearing towards you.

However greatly you may be held in honor, never cease to be aware of your position nor speak any word that is not to the king's taste. Do not persist when in argument with him; there is a proverb that he who argues with a king dies before his allotted time, and it is folly to thrust one's hand against an awl."

from A Mirror for Princes, *translated from the Persian by Reuben Levy (Dutton 1951)*

بیاراسته همچو خلد برین

همه شهر و کو و درو آفرین

زکشته درنیوز بدیوارها

جنهای گل کشته بازارها

زخفتان زربفت و خود کم

علم بسته در زوان زهاش نبرین

زدزوان ا شهر تا قصر شاه

نکند سقر لاطو اطلس را

همه شهر درزیوز زرنگان

زدویم درپای اسپان بشا

کجوز شاه زاده مؤید کاما

درعین جلادت و اقتدار

بمستقر سریر سلطنت قرار

یافت وان پیامن اواز داد

وضعف واثار رحمت

ومعدلت بی نهایت عرصه

دلکشای نوح اوزای سمر

که نزهتگاه شیرین لبان شکر

خته است غیر فردو بزبون

ورشک نگار خانه چین کشت

نظم

Firdausi took thirty-five years to complete the Shah Nameh, *or Book of Kings. He is shown in a later miniature (left of center) in an audience before his patron, Mahmud of Ghazni, to whom the book was dedicated.*

THE ART OF THE MINIATURE

The lovely Persian art of miniature painting owes its flowering to a religious taboo: the Islamic prohibition against representation of the human figure. A greater obstacle to painting can hardly be imagined, but it was precisely in the circumventing of this obstacle that the miniature flourished from its peak in the fifteenth century to the seventeenth. Because of the restriction, the old Persian instinct for decoration was given full scope, at the expense of figures. At the same time the painting was reduced to such a scale that it could be kept discreetly within the covers of a book.

Most miniaturists bred white cats, for their brushes were made from the throat hairs of two-month-old kittens. The hairs were bound with a silk thread and stuck in a pigeon quill, with a single hair protruding to make a tip. Colors were mineral, pounded and ground, then sifted through silk and mixed with a binder. Their papers were made of silk and linen rag polished with mother-of-pearl or a crystal egg.

The conventions of miniature art are strict, and often of Chinese origin. There is no perspective and no shading but rather a two-dimensional scene usually viewed from a slight elevation. The artists had little regard for scale, sometimes painting a man larger than a camel and always making a noble taller than his servants. They used colors not for natural representation but for their own aesthetic value, turning lions pink and trees orange as their fancies urged.

The backgrounds of miniatures are of two kinds—landscape and architecture. The latter are no more than stage sets, screens folded around or behind the action. Their beauty is mainly the beauty of composition. The landscapes, on the other hand, are, by their nature, less formal and their beauty is entirely romantic. They are gorgeously colored, embroidered cloths flung against the world, showing the horizon only at the very top.

Costume, accoutrements, hints at gestures, grouping, all gently indicate the story which is being illustrated. Drama and emotion, particularly in the faces, are abjured, for that would disturb the tranquillity which most miniatures intend, and also by so humanizing the figures the artists would have further transgressed the Islamic prohibition. These are the impersonal groupings of ballet, not the protagonists of drama.

Miniaturists found their inspiration in the poems of the Sufi mystics and in tales of the Arab lovers Laila and Majnun, but their chief source was the Shah Nameh, *or Book of Kings, recounting Persia's history from the legendary hero Rustam to the last Sasanian king. Written by Firdausi, and first published in 1010, it has been called "the only early history ever read or believed by Persians."*

The following selection of miniatures, although painted intentionally in the Timurid style, is taken from a Shah Nameh *of 1614. Commissioned by Shah Abbas the Great, the Safavid ruler in Isfahan (see page 69), it is now a treasure of the Spencer Collection of the New York Public Library.*

Siyawush, a pre-Achaemenid prince (left, foreground) plays polo at the Turanian court. This royal sport developed in Persia, spreading first to the East and only in the last century to the West.

The preparations for the coronation of Kai Khosrau, another ruler of prehistory, involve traditional Persian crafts. From upper right: spinning, weaving, engraving, forging, metalworking.

The hunt was a favorite sport of the Sasanian kings. Here Bahram V, called "Gur," who ruled A.D. 420–440, indulges a whim of his lute-playing mistress, Azada, to pin the hoof of a deer to its ear with an arrow.

Khosrau II, called "Parviz," the last great Sasanian king, visits the Armenian princess Shirin. The limpid pool, flowers, trees, and tiled façades make a perfect setting for Persian hospitality.

TEXT CONTINUED FROM PAGE 57

origin in a much earlier period, for we know from Saint Augustine and others that the Manichaean books of the Sasanian epoch were lavishly illustrated, but they reached their peak of perfection in the late fifteenth century.

Two conditions were necessary for the full development of the art. One was the existence of an ample literature, for miniatures after all are illustrations. This condition was met during the Timurid period by an avalanche of both epic and lyric poetry. The lyric poets—Saadi, Rumi, Hafiz, Jami—were inspired mainly by a new Persian religious movement, the mystical cult of Sufism. But the miniaturists found their chief source of material in the work of Persia's greatest epic poet, Firdausi.

The squire of a small village in Khurasan, Firdausi needed money for his daughter's dowry and for this reason accepted the patronage of the Turk, Mahmud of Ghazni (page 62). Thirty-five years later he had produced fifty thousand verses recounting the lives of fifty kings; the *Shah Nameh,* or Book of Kings, the Persian national epic, had been created and the little squire from Khurasan had become his country's Homer. The underlying theme of the *Shah Nameh* is the fight of heroes, notably Rustam, against the forces of darkness, the old Zoroastrian concept of the eternal battle between good and evil. Today, almost a thousand years later, its verses are known to every Persian peasant.

The second condition necessary for the full development of the miniature art was a sustained and sympathetic patronage. This the miniaturists found in the Il-Khan and Timurid dynasties created by the Mongol invasions of the thirteenth and fourteenth centuries. It was said of Genghis Khan, the first of the Mongols in Persia, that he was born with a clot of blood in his fist. Certainly he and his successors, Hulagu Khan and Tamerlane, leveled buildings and stacked skulls in almost every town they conquered. Yet their invasions were not entirely destructive, and even their severest critics admit that it was ordinarily their practice to spare scholars, artists, and poets.

The greatest of these patrons were the Timurids. The founder of the dynasty, Tamerlane, who claimed descent from Genghis Khan, was born in Kesh, "the green city," not far from Samarkand. Early in his youth his mother died and his father went into seclusion, leaving Tamerlane to his favorite pursuits: chess, polo, and stealing sheep. From a wound received in a local rebellion he gained his sobriquet, Timur the Lame, and, as Tamerlane, went on to conquer twenty-seven Asian kingdoms and to make himself master of the Moslem world. Both brigand and connoisseur, he took scholars and painters along on his violent campaigns, and when he found artists of talent, he would ship them back like loot to his beloved Samarkand. His successors showed similar extremes of temperament. Gowhar Shad, Tamerlane's daughter-in-law, is famous for the magnificent mosque she ordered built at Mashad and for the vicious intrigues that led to her execution at the age of eighty. The Timurid prince

The Sound of Persian

More than one hundred fifty English words have been borrowed from the Persian. In his excellent short book The Splendor of Persia *(Alfred A. Knopf, 1957) Robert Payne offers the following list of sixty, and proposes: "If you will say some of these words softly, with a slight sing-song intonation, you will have some idea of the sound of Persian."*

azure	jasmine	naphtha	satrap
bazaar	jasper	narcissus	scarlet
candy	julep	orange	scimitar
caravan	jungle	palanquin	seersucker
cheque	khaki	paradise	shawl
chess	lemon	peach	sherbet
cinnabar	lilac	peacock	spinach
cypress	lime	pear	sugar
dervish	Magi	puttee	taffeta
divan	magic	pajama	tapestry
exchequer	margarine	rice	tiara
gazelle	marguerite	rook	tiger
henna	muscadel	saccharine	tulip
jackal	musk	saffron	turban
jargon	myrtle	sash	verandah

Hussein Bayqara was known for his inordinate love of fighting cocks and rams and for his patronage of the mystical poet Jami and Bihzad, the best of the Persian miniaturists. One would not suppose that the Timurids did much for the moral tone of their age, but without them Persian art would be like the Renaissance without the Medici.

An eminent student of Persian art has said that, to the kings and nobles for whom the miniatures were created, painting was no more than an opportunity for relaxation. The charge may well be true. Several years ago a friend and I had occasion to visit an old nobleman who lived in the north of Persia. When we called, he was out, and we were led to an *ivan*, a recessed porch, to await his return. In the center of the *ivan* there was a small star-shaped pool from which water flowed in tiled channels down the hollowed-out balustrades of a flight of steps and on into a second pool, which stretched the length of the garden. It was good to see so much water after a day in a jeep on the desert.

After a short time a woman servant came out bringing us big glasses of ice cold *sharbat*, which is a kind of mild fruit punch. This woman in her youth had been our host's mistress, and it was said that then she had the most beautiful eyebrows in the kingdom. Now she was old and large, veiled, slung with jewels, and barefoot. Before we had finished the *sharbat*, she was out again, this time with a leather album under her arm. It was a portfolio of miniatures.

My friend and I hitched our chairs together and opened the folio out on our knees. The first page, except for the area of the miniature insert, was patterned all over in cream and gold, and suggested what Persians would call a paradise, a park or garden full of animals and birds. The miniature showed a king and his courtiers in a garden. Against a foreground of cinnamon brown there were groups of cooks, musicians, and courtiers dressed in robes of red, green, black, and yellow. At the bottom cooks turned kabob on a spit under a flowering tree. Above them—and not behind, due to the absence of a third dimension—musicians played small heart-shaped lutes, and one banged on a tambourine whose circle was repeated in the platters spread around on the ground. Yet another tier up were the courtiers, sashed in gold, wearing big floppy turbans of gold, the latter making patterns of form as well as of color. Finally, above all was the king curled up on his golden throne, a kind of canopied, eight-sided bed, cushioned in green, the top in red.

The next page depicted a battle. Little warriors on ponies like rocking horses were frozen in a gallop across a salmon-colored plain. My friend was pointing out some odd bit of detail when our host walked in. He was a tall, straight, old man of about eighty with a rose in his buttonhole and a very elegant mustache. Out of politeness it is customary for educated Persians to greet and speak to foreign guests in either French or English, but our host saluted us in Persian and with one of the more elaborate Persian greetings. If he had known, he said, that we were coming, he would have planted our way with flowers. Then he switched to English, an English he had learned from a tutor at the age of ten and had improved upon by frequenting the court of George V. So we liked his poor, miserable selection of miniatures. Then we should see some more.

Our host flickered through the pages of the second album as one might flick through the pages of a magazine, but now and then he would rub the creamy stuff of the paper between his fingers or touch gently with his finger tips the top of a painting. Something in his manner set me to thinking of the Timurids, one of whom perhaps had commissioned some of the miniatures we were looking at. I thought of the big folios slipped into their velvet cases and packed on a mule along with the picnic hampers, the tents and carpets, the creels of wine. I pictured Bayqara under a tree with his miniatures, enjoying them as my host enjoyed them now.

I began to realize that the servant had brought us the miniatures not because she had thought we were students of the art—as indeed we were not—but because she had thought we were tired, that we might want simply to relax with beauty. When we left, the old prince bowed and touched his heart and told us that by our presence we had made his house a garden.

The brilliant but unstable Timurids were able to maintain their rule in Persia for little more than a century and a half. In 1500, weakened by domestic struggles for power, they were overthrown. The new rulers, who had first to throw back an invasion of Uzbeks from the north, were the Safavids. They owed their success to the fact that they were Persians and to the fact that they were the champions of the Shia sect, the interpretation of Islam that had always been popular in Persia. Twice before—under the Achaemenids and the Sasanians—national regeneration had been accompanied by a rebirth of religion. Now once again, after eight hundred years, Persia was united and grew powerful under a dynasty of Persian kings who were as well the protagonists of a national religion.

The Safavids pushed the boundaries of Persia out to correspond roughly with those of Sasanian times, and the coun-

TEXT CONTINUED ON PAGE 72

Shah Abbas, here seen hawking, was the greatest of the Safavid rulers. He drove the Ottomans from Persian soil, established maritime relations with Europe, and made of his capital city a garden spot so beautiful that Persians still say "Half the world is Isfahan." At left the Masjid-i-Shah rises above the main square, its mosaic dome gleaming against the sheer, barren mountains.

OVERLEAF: *The art of rug making, which Shah Abbas patronized in the royal ateliers at Isfahan, flourishes today on a commercial basis. Some of the modern products, newly washed, are spread out to dry on the cliffs of Cheshmeh-Ali, near Teheran, above a heroic carving of the Qajar king Fath Ali Shah and his court.*

OVERLEAF: *Paris-Match*

69

TEXT CONTINUED FROM PAGE 69

try became such a power that even the Ottoman Turks were contained. Internally the country prospered; once again it became a halfway house of trade between East and West. Much of the physical damage done by the Mongols was repaired and an extensive program of public works was completed. The most lasting contribution of the Safavids, however, lay in the capital they created at Isfahan, in central Persia. Mainly the work of Shah Abbas the Great, it remains today one of the most beautiful cities in the East.

Isfahan is an oasis. Blessed by temperate seasons, watered in abundance by the river Zayanda Rud, it has been famous always for its gardens and its fruit. Here in the center of the oasis Abbas laid out a square, today the second largest in the world (after Red Square in Moscow). It is surrounded by a continuous wall of arches, the largest of which frame the royal mosque at one end, the royal bazaar at the other. On the eastern side of the square, Abbas built for his father-in-law, Sheik Lutf Ullah, a small mosque that is one of the masterpieces of Persian architecture. To stand beneath its perfect dome is to stand at the heart of a colored crystal. Opposite, across the square, there is a massive gatehouse, topped with a deep porch pillared like an Achaemenid hall. Beyond the gate lay the king's palaces, his gardens, and the workshops of his artists: the potters and tile-makers, the miniaturists and bookbinders, the weavers and metalworkers. Here too, in the seventeenth century, were produced fine examples of what is perhaps the most quintessential of the Persian arts, the carpet.

For a Persian there has never been any possession more precious. Carpets were the principal appointment in both the palace and the house. Their portability made them practical furnishings for the tent as well as for gardens and pavilions. Often, too, they were hung from balconies or across bare façades. Finally, it is on a carpet that a Persian prays.

Most carpets are meant to represent a garden. The English word "paradise" is of Persian derivation and its original meaning in Persian is "garden." Indeed for a Persian a garden is synonymous with perfect bliss. We hear of Cyrus setting out an orchard with his own hand, of Xerxes while on campaign hanging a tree with golden ornaments in tribute to its beauty, of courtiers drinking wine out of large bowls during the rose season, "for the rose is a guest for only forty days." It was natural that the garden should have become the model for their most treasured art.

A carpet has a border as a garden has a wall. Within the center medallion it often has a pool, representing the eternal pool of heaven. In between there are other garden motifs: the palmette, a lotus or peony seen in profile; the rosette, any open, petaled flower viewed straight on; the arabesque, a convoluted vine ending in a trumpetlike blossom. Finally there is a motif that looks like a curl or loop of ribbon and is called a cloud band. Chinese by origin, it became popular with the Persians because, like the flowing arabesque but

unlike the static palmette and stellate forms, it quickens the design with motion. In the case of hunting carpets, small animal and human figures were added to these basic motifs. Prayer carpets incorporate a *mihrab*, showing the direction of Mecca. With the great carpets of the sixteenth and early seventeenth centuries, the brilliant history of Persian art reaches its last climax.

In the eighteenth century four different dynasties attempted to rule Persia. The Afghans invaded and, after a horrible siege of Isfahan, deposed the Safavids. A Persian named Nadir Shah drove out the Afghans, established his own house, and was assassinated. After a period of anarchy the humane and civilized Zands appeared, but they were overthrown in 1794 by the Qajars. With the Qajars came peace but little honor, for throughout the nineteenth century and into the twentieth they ruled Persia mainly for the benefit of the Russians and the British. The powers of the modern world were drawn to Persia by the same magnets that drew the ancient invaders: her strategic location and her treasure —once gold, now oil. As Western arms and bribes posed a threat to Persia's national sovereignty, so Western manufactured goods posed a subtler threat to her cultural integrity. With what pride did Lord Curzon, the Viceroy of India, visiting the Isfahan bazaar in 1890, report the array of products from the looms of Manchester! As Arthur Upham Pope, the greatest Western authority on the art of Persia, has said: "The Mongol barbarians learned more quickly to appreciate the excellencies of the indigenous art than did the self-satisfied commercial West."

But Persia is more than a moonlit ruin enchanted with memories of jeweled courts and magic swords. In the two shahs of the Pahlavi line, who threw out the corrupt Qajars and set Persia on the road to modernization, it is not fanciful to see some of the strength of the ancient kings. The lean, taut, Persian face, with a glint of wild magic (magic is a Persian word, from the Magi, who were Persian, too), is the same face that is carved on the stones of Persepolis. The average Persian is still a lover of strength (he likes to toss dumbbells in the ancient ritual sport of the *zurkhaneh*) and of poetry (Radio Teheran begins each day with verses from Firdausi) and of beauty in all its forms. Beneath the widespread poverty and corruption of present-day Persia, the Persian still holds in his heart a love for the qualities that made this land a place of splendor and a home of glory. Once, walking in a park at Isfahan, a gardener pointed out to me an ox of a man carrying a load of brick. "He is the knight of this garden," he said. "Why?" I asked. "Because," he replied, "he is strong and clever and very good." It was an answer straight from the *Shah Nameh*.

Terence O'Donnell has been most recently a Fulbright lecturer at the University of Isfahan. His article "Evenings at the Bridge" appeared in the May, 1961, issue of HORIZON.

By MURRAY KEMPTON

BLAKE HAMPTON

THE ARTIST IN OUR TIME

OR: SOME NOTES ON THE UNFORTUNATE CONSEQUENCES

OF HAVING GIVEN MR. WHISTLER AN OPENING

Our century may have begun with the lady who told James McNeill Whistler that, in matters of art, she at least knew what she liked—and was incinerated on the spot when he answered that this, Madame, was a capacity shared by all the higher animals. The self-assurance of bad private taste thereupon surrendered to official authority and, for a few unreal moments, the artist was officially in charge. It was of course too good a place for servants to keep, and the artists gave it over almost at once to the critics, who have since given most of it over to the publishers and art dealers.

Mrs. John F. Kennedy walks our National Gallery in the company of André Malraux, the French Minister of Culture. When they have finished, the journalists ask the great critic what paintings pleased him. He dismisses the new Copley, which the evidence would indicate that Mrs. Kennedy had previously known she liked. He mentions the El Greco *Laocoön,* the Veneziano *St. John,* the two Neroccio portraits. When he has finished, the journalists ask Mrs. Kennedy what she has liked. "I like," she answers, "whatever he likes." She is at once a great lady with a guest, and a woman of the age in which Authority is the guest of honor.

Whistler's victory over the amateur Philistines seems to have been permanent. In organized battalions they have dared since to return only in the disguise of critics and artists. When a president of the United States (not the present one) described abstract expressionism as what

73

might happen when an artist threw an egg at the canvas, the educated public immediately felt its alienation from a man with so deficient an appreciation for what it had been told it liked. We take what we are told to take.

In the higher reaches of art the informed public is anxious to please. The critics are haunted enough by the mistakes of their predecessors to protect themselves against history's reproach by careful sympathy for anything that is new. All in all, we would seem to be in an ideal period for the experimental artist. Unfortunately for the artist, however, sympathy has turned out to be a worse enemy than affront. The power to shock convention no longer exists in any substantial form. Convention has become an audience watching and occasionally applauding. The path of the revolutionary ends in the studio with David Susskind and that smile mixing hate with a desperation to understand and sympathize. Convention wants so much to understand that it no longer looks and listens.

The artistic rebel is now the adolescent in the American family. There are few material positions more enviable than this: the basic hostility of the adult is suppressed, the allowance is assured. Middle age has to believe that youth is the future and that the future, in and of itself, will be an improvement. We expect alienation and rebellion; we have raised our children to be our judges and to correct our mistakes. When Barry Goldwater, Jr., announces his interest in enlisting in the Peace Corps, his father, who voted against it, discovers that he has always been for it; in the same style, the best way to get a grant from an academy is to be studiously nonacademic.

The immense discussion aroused by the Beat movement in literature seems in fact to have been due less to the products of its leaders than to their talent for acting out adolescence in public. They were above all performers and playing a part that would have been impossible a generation ago, when parents told children not to be forward in company. Allen Ginsberg was the public image of adolescent pain; Gregory Corso, the public image of adolescent buffoonery. What they published was only their homework, and their elders, once assured that their homework was done, were chiefly interested in their after-school activities.

These activities, not being of the wholesome outdoor kind, soon became a trial to our patience. They were middle-class young men of the sort whose parents one knows, but whose attentions to one's daughter are an impossible peril, the adolescent boy the neighbors think should be shipped off to school. And Ginsberg, Corso, and Jack Kerouac seem always to be going away to prep school—Paris, Tangier, or Mexico, any place the chief asset of which is the promise of isolation from the community. In Kerouac's case, at least, the adolescent goes with an impressive allowance from his parent, Society. There seems always to be an editor who will pay Kerouac to get out of town. His letters home sound as they always did, but the distance of the postmark is reassuring.

These are the naughty brothers. They have proper ones—a little pallid but attentive to their studies. The latter can go to graduate school, where their disciplines, being useless, are seldom asked about but, being inoffensive, are respected in the family. One thinks of the young American composer, trained in the classical tradition

but beating feebly and without disruptive passion to escape from it. His place is in the university and his presence is part of its distinction: every little college has its record library but only a great institution can have a composer-in-residence. He is uncomplaining, like most proper children; occasionally he is rewarded by the performance of one of his works—that is, he is given a party and a handsome one when you consider union scale. These rare feast days are cherished in his memory and forgotten by the family; his party is not the sort to produce anecdotes. He is otherwise the least noticed family member; no one is ashamed of him, but no one really knows what he is doing, either.

The painter is a brother with more substance, if only because he offers the chance of capital gain. Every American knows at least two things about art: Pablo Picasso paints women with six noses, and Pablo Picasso has twelve bank accounts. Any doubts aroused about the logic of the Picasso of the first legend are overwhelmingly refuted by the Picasso of the second. The painter is the brother who might pay back his allowance with interest. The art market is a woman who wants a fashionable painting, acting in concert with a husband whom she has managed to convince that a painting is as sound as real estate. And, in any art, the dealer and the critic reach their most awesome authority when they can establish themselves as investment counselors. To consider what one likes in painting has become, not merely a social embarrassment but, what is just a little bit worse, a potential economic miscalculation.

All of this would be pleasant and comparatively comfortable—with large and necessary exceptions—if, as the lady said to Henry James about Mr. Ruskin, the subject were not *"Art!"* But then, when we surrendered the option to like what we chose to like, we gained humility at the price of enthusiasm.

The twentieth century may also have begun when the young Marcel in *The Guermantes Way* was riding home from the evening at the Duchess's, for which he had yearned since adolescence, and heard his interior voice asking: "Is *that* all there is?" The dream that every man had the right to some full and rich experience in life was the democratic invention of the nineteenth century; disappointment with that moment, once achieved, was the democratic experience of the twentieth. We are hardly the most bored society in history, but we must be the first to feel cheated by boredom.

The public's toleration of the artist is that boredom's reflection. Men do not abdicate their taste to other men if their taste is a matter of great importance to them. The gift of toleration is the highest within boredom's range. To say that the artist is no longer able to affront is to say that he is no longer able to involve.

But the wistful sense that art ought to mean pleasure is stubborn if dim. Not in spite of being bored, but because we are, we still demand that the artist tell us a story. When his product no longer tells us a story, we demand that he do so himself in the manner of his living and dying. The artist takes the fall for his art.

All these conditions, I think, go to account for the vast amount of conversation about, if not lasting attention to, American jazz. The jazz musician is fashionable, at least as symbol, which seems rather odd when you consider how close he is to the artist of tradition. Jazz has a smaller public than Europe must think, but it is certainly better trained and essentially more engaged than the audience for "action" painting. The music is produced by entirely professional men, devoted to one another and united against the public and the critics. They work to communicate, at least with one another; their work disturbs occasionally, but it disturbs something in the listener's interior. They avoid the freakish; there is really no jazz Dada.

The jazz community thus has the qualifications that men used to employ when they described any serious artistic school. It is also fortunate in having certain standards, which could hardly be said for painting since that historic spring of 1959 when the Museum of Modern Art offered an exhibit of sixteen new painters that included a young man whose inner voice had told him to paint American flags, one distinguishable from another only by size and frame.

The very largeness of spirit and fidelity to his community that sets the jazz musician apart from other artists is peculiarly tragic because of the narrow proportions of his form. His own desires and the pretensions of his cult are limitless, but their form is a prison. He tries, when he is most serious, continually to break out of it. The history of jazz is full of escape attempts, most of them unfortunate. Bix Beiderbecke's experiments in the twenties all ended in pale Debussy; a generation later Lester Young was saying that he might do something truly memorable if only some promoter would record him with a great string orchestra. Both had done memorable things before; but when each thought of the permanent, each thought of the classical tradition.

But the limitations of his medium aside, the jazz musician is the archetype of the artist in our time because he alone fills our lingering need to think of the artist as always struggling, always defeated. The idea of someone dying in our place and leaving us behind to feel sorry for ourselves must go back to the beginning of speech, but its application to the artist seems really to have become general in the nineteenth century, which was the first to offer the chance that every Western white man could have enough to eat.

Our society is one peculiarly empty of intimate hazard. We may all be subject to general annihilation, but it is a danger distant, impersonal, and therefore but dimly imagined. Men often go bankrupt; they never go hungry. Police are gentle with alcoholics if they are white and have neckties. The diseases are controlled: our poets die old. The most common task is the shuffling of paper. Even the traditional sins are hardly subject to notice: we are fascinated by homosexuality and narcotics because adultery and alcoholism are so commonplace.

The jazz musician stands then as the only artist who, by class, can be described as an outsider. The most important reason for this is that he generally is a Negro and therefore automatically an outsider. Some persons who are not Negroes occasionally wish they were, a desire that a Negro can summon up only by rigorous intellectual effort. It is a dreadful thing to be half a servant and half a heroic myth. The argument as to whether jazz is essentially a Negro expression is settled by the condition that it is a Negro job. Even if he is white, the strangers who are his customers feel free to call any jazz musician by his first name.

Doom is the appointed destiny of the outsider, for whom the family can feel pity but not loss. He is expected to suffer and die as substitute. The jazz musician's votaries seem in fact to have a certain impatience with him if he persists in physical survival. What is hard reality to him is delightful fantasy to them. Of course, only persons denied suffering really miss it; Van Gogh had his deficiencies of taste, but who could imagine him enjoying *Lust for Life*? Our Van Gogh figure is the jazz musician; Charlie Parker is the subject of at least two novels and four short stories fleshing out the poverty of his medium with the supposed romance of his environment.

Jazz has a whole cult of the dead. Its hagiography requires not merely a poverty-stricken end but a horrible one; the myth is always the sordid or the frustrated—Bessie Smith dying because the white hospital would not take her, Beiderbecke cracking in the search for the note that was not there, Parker thrown anonymously on a slab in the mortuary. King Oliver, on the other hand, died shabby but with dignity; he is respected but no saint.

Miss Billie Holliday has a particular place in this shrine because she died by slow stages and in public. Her last years were in fact nearly an exercise in relic display. She *was* a relic, of course, as a performer, but her managers were almost careful to see that she filled the role. Her audience could look at her and reflect on the consequences of sexual abuse and heroin and Jim Crow and other delightful experiences against which they were so well protected. It was more comfortable to see her ruined than to see her intact.

For there is a little something in us all that hates the artist and wants him dead. The jazz musician is the only artist who can offer his public the prospect of that consolation, and that is one reason he has a public.

Nothing offers the tension that used to exist between the artist and his audience quite so well as the spectacle of Miles Davis at work in a night club. Davis's distaste for his audience is constantly just this side of open insult. Yet the audience forgives him everything and not because it knows him, in private moments, to be a pleasant and intelligent young man. He is not really pardoned his manners. The audience merely postpones its vengeance, because it knows that someday he will get His from the Enemy and that his audience never will. The cops who merely chase college students when they are loud will beat up Miles Davis just for standing there. He is especially interesting therefore to persons who have appointed him to take their place as victims of society.

So only the jazz musician still has an audience with important elements of the Philistine, if the word be defined in its only sensible meaning, which is hostility to the artist. Perhaps there can be no real audience that does not have this element. Any involvement carries with it a measure of dislike. Nowadays most artists are protected from such dangerous involvement by a combination of public subsidy and public indifference. There must, of course, be moments when some artist envies the old order where the jazz musician lives still in the old isolation. It is misplaced envy. We all admire James Joyce more than we do Hugh Walpole; but, if Joyce had had common sense, he would far rather have been Walpole.

Murray Kempton has been a columnist for the New York Post *since 1949, and is the author of* Part of Our Time. *Next month he will become Editor-at-Large of* The New Republic.

FRED PLAUT

Although it looks like a diagram of the *Fail-Safe* point, the chart below is, in fact, no more sinister than a page from *J. S. Bach or* Le Sacre du Printemps. *It was used by composer Lukas Foss (right) and his three colleagues as a guide for one of their exercises in collective improvisation. Conventional notation is useless for music that is more or less made up as they go along, but a chart such as this can assign priorities to the various instruments and indicate the shape of the piece, if not its content. At the end, the percussion moves in from the background and takes over:* CLASH—*silence.*

Some of the most arresting music heard in today's concert halls is being invent

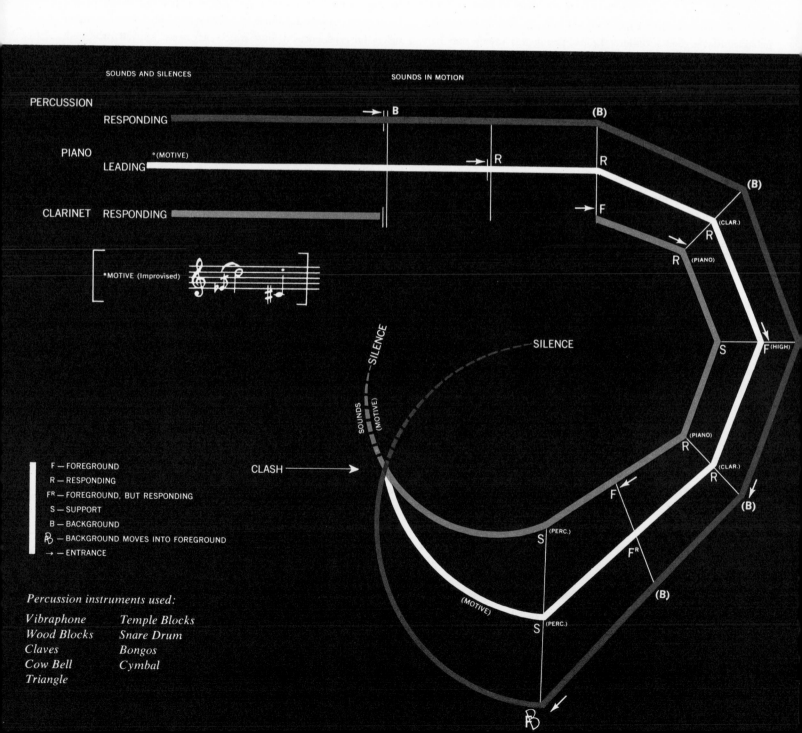

AND NOW

THE

ATONAL

AD LIB

the spot by Lukas Foss and his chamber ensemble   *By* ALFRED FRANKENSTEIN

Lukas Foss, composer, conductor, pianist, and professor of music at the University of California in Los Angeles, is, in all likelihood, the only man in history who ever induced a philanthropic foundation to create and maintain a set of rivals to himself.

These rivals were two groups of musical improvisers, established in 1960 to serve as goad and gadfly to Foss's own Improvisation Chamber Ensemble. They are no longer active because jobs and the draft drained their personnel away, but new competing groups are bound to come into being at Foss's headquarters on the U.C.L.A. campus if not elsewhere; improvisation is much in the wind and forms an important chapter in the theory and practice of today's avant-garde.*

For the past quarter of a century American cultural historians have dwelt on collective improvisation in jazz, seeing it as a phenomenon peculiar to American life, while often neglecting to add that collective improvisation is also characteristic of much Oriental and Gypsy music, and that it was not unknown to Johann Sebastian Bach and his times; Foss, however, does not see his own work against a background of such precedents, in which long-lingering elements of folk tradition play a significant role, but rather as parallel to the development of "aleatory" techniques by some of today's most advanced composers.

"Aleatory" is the latest catchword from European centers of musical experiment. It refers to chance or random procedures, of which many kinds are in use, some of them seemingly freakish or ironic in intent. For example, John Cage, the leading American exponent, may compose a piece—so he says—according to the graphic accidents of the sheet before him, allowing the spots, blotches, and other imperfections in the paper to determine

*See, for example, "Art by Accident" in HORIZON for September, 1960, and "After-Dark Satire Goes to Town" in the issue of January, 1962.

where he puts his notes. The French composer Pierre Boulez has produced a piano-sonata movement with each page of the score split horizontally into three sub-pages, printed on both sides; these sub-pages may be combined and recombined in various different ways, like the leaves of those children's picture books in which, at the flip of a finger, the body of a bear may be given the head of a zebra at one moment and the head of a camel at another. It is also very common for these composers to indicate general areas of pitch rather than a specific pitch, and some of their music, whether its pitch be fixed or not, is printed on unbound sheets of paper which need not follow each other in any established order. Some of these pages, indeed, may be left out altogether, and Cage has even gone so far as to suggest in certain instances that *everything* be left out.

Except for the first, all of these aleatory procedures establish a creative partnership between composer and player but limit its exercise to the moment of performance. They developed partly in reaction to and partly as a result of total serialism, the most rigidly controlled technique in the history of music.

The underlying philosophy of total serialism is easily enough explained, although its application in the individual instance may be very difficult to analyze. Its purpose is to impose form on the atonal chaos that results from rejecting the discipline of specific keys—as Arnold Schoenberg was the first to do—and giving all twelve tones of the octave equal importance. To this end, orthodox serialism submits the development of a musical composition to a formula. The twelve notes within the octave are rearranged by the composer to form a sort of theme, which is called a "tone-row." Out of this the composition is built. The notes may be used horizontally as melody or piled up vertically in chords, but only in the order established by the tone-row; furthermore, all twelve notes in the series must be employed before any can be repeated. For greater variety, the tone-row may also be presented upside down, backwards, or both backwards and upside down, but the same rigorous principles apply. And in total serialism every aspect of musical composition—pitch, rhythm, dynamics, instrumentation, spacing, tempo, and so on—is similarly determined by a prearranged set of relationships.

These controlling relationships can even be coded and fed into an electronic computer, and an electronic computer, under the gentle prodding of Lejaren A. Hiller and Leonard M. Isaacson, has actually "composed" a string quartet. The irony of total serialism is that in demanding that every element of music be ruled by a predetermined order, it leads music further and further away from aural considerations. What is on paper the most highly organized music ever created often sounds totally *dis*organized; the more implacably systematized the music becomes, the closer it seems to approach a completely random state so far as the listener's ear is concerned.

In total serialism the performer has neither freedom nor responsibility; he simply follows the score. In most aleatory music, on the other hand, the performer does have freedom, but, in Foss's view, it is freedom only to act irresponsibly and to no very significant end. If it makes no difference whether one page or another is played, then the player makes no real contribution to the total effect by selecting one sequence of pages as against another; it is all likely to come out very much the same no matter how it is shuffled. Such, at least, is the opinion of Lukas Foss, German-born but for twenty years one of America's most prolific composers and now, at forty, one of its most inventive as well.

It should be added here that aleatory composers, almost to a man, are devotees of electronic music, although they write for the traditional instruments as well. Electronic music is the particular haven of chance or random effect, and electronic music, be it well noted, eliminates the performer entirely. Foss, however, gives the performer a new, vital, and unprecedented role.

Foss's experiments with collective improvisation began, in fact, with dissatisfaction over the training of performing musicians today—what he regards as their inability (except for the jazzmen) really to hear each other and to adjust and respond to each other easily and elastically. So Foss embarked on improvisations with some of his students, and very quickly developed so emphatic a reaction from students and listeners alike that the next step was the establishment of an ensemble as a concert-giving institution.

The original Improvisation Chamber Ensemble, organized in 1957, consisted of six players. The group now contains four—Foss, pianist; Richard Dufallo, clarinetist; Charles Delancey, percussionist; and Howard Colf, cellist. Dufallo, Delancey, and Colf were pupils of Foss at U.C.L.A.; the first two are now among his faculty associates there, while Colf is a member of the Los Angeles Philharmonic. The combination of piano, clarinet, cello, and percussion assures a maximum of coloristic variety, especi-

ally since the percussionist commands a wide range of instruments—vibraphone, xylophone, and every imaginable type of bell, cymbal, gong, and drum. But instrumental color was only a secondary consideration in leading Foss to select these men; he chose them primarily for their gifts as performers and creators, as he chose the personnel of the rival groups now disbanded. (Each of these rival groups contained a singer; I have heard tapes of them, tapes that will probably be available on the commercial market before long, and it is indeed an experience to hear Foss's countertenor improvise an atonal song in that clear, honey-colored, sexless voice on the old Italian madrigal text *Dolcissima mia vita.*)

The Ensemble's style—the type of music it creates, its methods of rehearsal, its approach to the problem of form—has changed enormously during its brief existence; it is proper that an organization devoted to musical fluidity should itself remain fluid. There is, however, a general drift in the changes that have taken place.

Foss was a pupil of Paul Hindemith, the archenemy of atonality and serial techniques of every kind. Foss's own earlier music —there was much of it, and it was well received—was tonal, brilliant, dramatic, and colorful. One thinks of his cantata *The Prairie* (composed when he was nineteen), his four settings of *The Song of Songs,* his String Quartet in G (1947), his *Parable of Death* (1952) for tenor, narrator, mixed chorus, and orchestra, with texts by Rainer Maria Rilke; it was all the work of a skilled conservative with something to say. Through improvisation, however, he has become more and more interested in one serial procedure, the twelve-tone row, which predetermines pitch relationships but leaves rhythm, dynamics, tempo, and all the rest to be handled freely. Nowadays Foss will give entire programs with the Improvisation Chamber Ensemble without once venturing into conventional tonality. For this reason the Ensemble's phonograph record, *Studies in Improvisation* (RCA Victor LM-2558), does not represent its latest thinking, for much of it is in specific keys. Far more typical of the newer trend, and most extraordinary both in form and effect, is Foss's recorded *Time Cycle* (Columbia ML-5680/MS-6280), for soprano voice and symphony orchestra, with improvised interludes played by Foss and his three associates between the scored portions for voice and orchestra. This composition is largely atonal, but its last movement contains an all but uniquely successful effort to reconcile tonality and the twelve-tone row.*

His *Time Cycle* also exists in a version for voice and the four instruments of the Ensemble, without symphony orchestra, since Foss likes to contrast composition—planned in detail, studiously organized, employing carefully calculated climaxes and returns

---

*It has also been uniquely successful in stirring some of today's audiences out of their lethargy. On the occasion of the Boston première of *Time Cycle,* William Henry Chamberlin reported that there was "such a noticeable stampede for the exits that references to the mass withdrawal appeared in the notices of the concert." Those reviews included such comment as "Way out and queer stuff. . . . Felt like the struggle for the last lifeboat on a sinking liner. . . . The entire Boston Symphony Orchestra was made to sound like a chamber group as it twittered, plunked, twanged, and honked."

—with the spontaneity of improvisation, and he often includes some examples of composition on the Ensemble's programs. When I first heard him, in 1959, he presented a concerto for the Ensemble with orchestra; the Ensemble's part was improvised, the orchestra's was played from score. Nowadays he does not combine the genres in that way, but is likely to devote separate parts of the program to each.

He insists upon calling his improvisations studies in texture, and he sometimes calls them studies in collective composition as well. These improvised pieces demand infinitely more rehearsal than written music. What the concertgoer hears is improvised, all well enough, but it is developed on the basis of innumerable run-throughs.

The traditional jazz musician starts with a tune and a chord pattern, and since these things do not change very much, a traditional jazz musician is at home anywhere in the world of his art—although, to be sure, jazzmen who have long worked together are likely to invent more daring collective effects than jazzmen who are new to each other. There are, however, no guest artists with the Improvisation Chamber Ensemble. No one could step in and join this group on the night of a performance. It simply doesn't work that way.

To begin with, Foss's Ensemble does not start from a tune or a chord pattern, although it may introduce a twelve-tone row during the course of a given piece, and in the improvised give-and-take among the players that twelve-tone row may be subjected to the classic inversion, retrogression, and retrograde inversion as well as to the classic transposition, augmentation, diminution, and shift from melodic to chordal forms. (All this, mind you, without benefit of the written note.) "Every piece must be about something," says Foss, and this implies that every piece must be about something different from every other piece. Some of the things the pieces were about when I heard the Ensemble rehearse in Los Angeles were runs (fast motion in scale-wise notes), jagged contours (which are the opposite of runs), fog, and the mocking of the cello by the clarinet. The last two sound like the descriptive, extra-musical ideas of old-fashioned "program music," and they are; but all these things are simply the germ cells from which an improvisation grows.

"Between the second and the third experiment with a given idea there may be no great degree of difference," says Foss, "but between the second and the twenty-second an entirely new piece usually emerges, one in which the original idea can no longer be recognized." What the public hears is the twenty-fifth or twenty-seventh version. This is no less an improvisation than the first, but it is infinitely subtler and more assured. Some of the Ensemble's admirers have wanted it to record two or three different improvisations on the same idea, but Foss resists this notion, with its implication that any one version is as good as any other; for him the improvisation is constantly being perfected until the idea wears out and is discarded. All the ideas on which Foss

erects his improvisations have a limited life span; when they no longer stimulate invention, they are put aside and new ones are taken up.

Since the traditional jazzman's understood tune and chord pattern, or anything remotely like it, will not work where there are neither tunes nor chords in the conventional sense, Foss and his associates have perennially sought some kind of notation, blueprint, chart, or memorandum to fall back on during improvisation. At one period, before they began to work atonally, they used a heavily condensed shorthand of ordinary staff notation, but this was not satisfactory. At another time they experimented briefly with words, which were intended to indicate the rhythm, accent, and pitch direction of the music. This, however, did not work any better. At the time this article was written they had evolved no rigid system that would cover all eventualities, but they were using charts employing a series of numbers to which special meanings were attached. These numbers, and what they are meant to indicate in Foss's wording, are as follows:

0 silence
1 thematic
2 responding (imitation)
3 isolated sustained notes
4 isolated notes of contrasting phrasing or dynamics
5 notes struck simultaneously
6 slow pulse
7 fast pulse
8 distant notes
9 design resulting from the interplay of isolated notes

Reproduced herewith is a portion of a chart based on these numerical symbols. The arrows, dots, and dashes in the middle have to do with passages of imitation between clarinet and cello ending with the cello's climbing, as indicated:

So simple a chart is particularly useful after the improvisation has been worked over to some extent. Foss also plots things on paper in greater detail, especially when an improvisation is just being launched. One of these plans, for the piece called *Runs,* reads, in part, as follows:

"1. PP. Order: percussion, clarinet, cello. Each plays until next comes in. Fades.

"Enter piano (out of time). First three entrances are signal for others to stop. *Fermata.* After that, continue exchanging undisturbed. Gong stroke starts

"2. PP. Percussion, clarinet, cello. Cello plays as before, but adding a sustained note (PP).

* * *

"7. A–A♭–F–F♯–B♭–G–E♭–D–B–C–E–D♭.

"On entrance of vibraphone and piano (PP), runs in dialogue (fast). Diverse or similar speed. Diverse or similar loudness. Clarinet and cello rows (slow). Do not stop as others enter, *fade*. . . .

"On entrance of

"8. Percussion, rumble (constant). Ascend slowly in even 16ths pulse. Crescendo.

"9. Highest pitch. Cello and clarinet. Steel. No pulse except once. Then percussion scraping or bounding. Then slow cello and clarinet descent (BRR . . .) PP. . . ." And so on.

This blueprint is not a miracle of verbal clarity or consistency, although some of its mysteries may be explained. The sequence of note-names at the head of section 7 is a twelve-tone row:

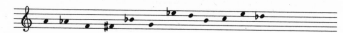

This can be turned upside down (inversion), each interval in the inverted form being a mirror image of the corresponding interval in the prime form:

The prime can also be played backwards (retrograde progression):

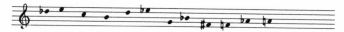

And so can the inversion (retrograde inversion):

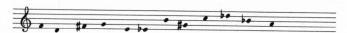

On the basis of these four forms of the row, an infinite variety of material can be improvised. It is rather surprising, in fact, to find Foss limiting his use of the row to only one of the ten sections of his piece, since the row—in general—is such a fecund device. One suspects that it must have been used in later sections of the improvisation as well, since there is nothing in the road-rules for these sections to prohibit it. In Section 9 the word "Steel" is meant to describe a peculiarly hard, cold, edgy quality of tone.

This chart prescribes a sequence of musical events with a very definite shape and order; but, except for the twelve-tone row, no specific notes are indicated. Rhythms, pulses, and paces are set forth, but there are no time signatures. The prescription is all to be filled out by the players as they improvise. As the players gain experience in following this pattern they will discard some solutions and retain others for further elaboration; furthermore the pattern itself will change gradually until ultimately an altogether new form will be arrived at. "The whole idea is to find new ways of listening to each other," says Foss. He alone seems to establish the original patterns for most of the improvisations involving the four instruments, but the final product is a totally collective one.

In the course of this work all concerned have learned endless new things about their own and each other's instruments. In fact, Foss thinks his whole concept of instrumentation has been revolutionized by this experience. When I visited the Ensemble at its headquarters in Los Angeles, I heard the clarinet and percussion embark on a duet in which the percussion was as liquid as any wood-wind instrument, and the clarinet as sharp and crackly as any instrument of percussion. I heard Charles Delancey strike his vibraphone with one of those bright little disc-shaped bells known as antique cymbals; both beater and beaten were sonorous bodies. Delancey and Foss were then working on a piece, since widely performed in public, in which both played the piano at once, the percussionist hitting the strings from the top with his sticks while the pianist used the keyboard in the usual manner.

Improvisation will create no masterpiece, Foss admits, but it will create a new type of musical literature, one which is none the less intense because it has been created only for the given moment and none the less creative for giving the performer rather than the composer the principal share in its existence. And by giving performers training in improvisation, Foss believes, one teaches them to find their way around in every kind of written music; they become in every way more alert, responsive, and adroit.

In general, it seems to me, Foss's claims are borne out by the music he makes with his associates Dufallo, Delancey, and Colf. To be sure, there is something risky about the whole thing, but risk is of its essence; the ideas don't always flow, but when they do flow, something dramatic happens—something wonderfully free in rhythm, and full of incredibly beautiful and highly original effects of color.

The Ensemble's worst fault is a certain preciousness that results from reaching too far for special effects, like making a kettledrum head vibrate in sympathy with a loudly blown note on the clarinet. Its greatest virtue is that it can transform its hearers into eager, active, excited participants in a total musical experience. The improvisations of jazz have been effecting that transformation for years, but to find it occurring in a non-jazz context is most unusual, to say the least. The atmosphere in a concert hall where Foss and his associates are playing is, most of the time, like the atmosphere in a ball park during the last half of the ninth inning, with the score tied, two men on base, and two out. This awakening, inspiriting, and revitalizing of the "classical" audience is the most remarkable thing with which the Improvisation Chamber Ensemble is to be credited.

Alfred Frankenstein is the music and art editor of the San Francisco Chronicle *and program annotator for the San Francisco Symphony. His books include* After the Hunt *and* Angels Over the Altar.

The rather unusual combination of instruments gives the Improvisation Chamber Ensemble a wide range of tonal color. Its members, from left to right, are: Howard Colf, cello; Lukas Foss, piano; Richard Dufallo, clarinet; and Charles Delancey, percussion. Below is still another type of chart used by the group, which in this case was augmented by a horn. In translating these symbols into sound, a player's task—Foss says—"is to listen critically" and "to find the appropriate note, rhythm, phrasing, dynamic, and register on his instrument—and at a moment's notice."

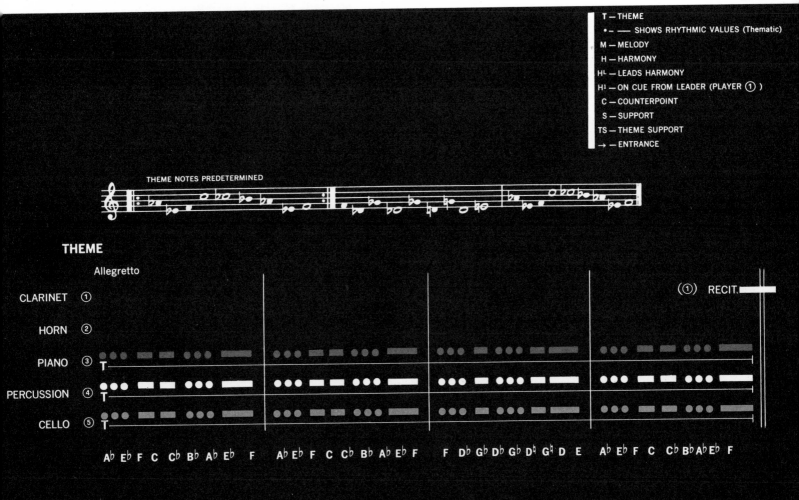

T — THEME
• — SHOWS RHYTHMIC VALUES (Thematic)
M — MELODY
H — HARMONY
HL — LEADS HARMONY
H¹ — ON CUE FROM LEADER (PLAYER ①)
C — COUNTERPOINT
S — SUPPORT
TS — THEME SUPPORT
→ — ENTRANCE

THEME NOTES PREDETERMINED

THEME

Allegretto

CLARINET ①   ① RECIT.

HORN ②

PIANO ③ T

PERCUSSION ④ T

CELLO ⑤ T

A♭ E♭ F C C♭ B♭ A♭ E♭ F   A♭ E♭ F C C♭ B♭ A♭ E♭ F   F D♭ G♭ D♭ G♭ D♭ G♭ D E   A♭ E♭ F C C♭ B♭ A♭ E♭ F

VARIATION I.—The piano and vibraphone exchange chords, back and forth, imitating the rhythmic pulse of the theme. The clarinet frames the variations with short, questioning recitative-phrases.

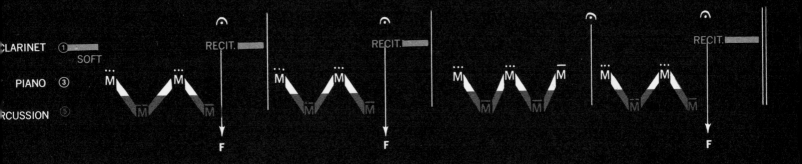

CLARINET ①   RECIT.   RECIT.   RECIT.
          SOFT

PIANO ③   M   M   M   M   M   W   M   M   M

PERCUSSION ⑤ M   M   M   M   M   M   M   M

F   F   F

By JAMES MORRIS

Is Oxford Out

Eight centuries of ivy and legend burden it.

Industrial smoke now overhangs it. Lost causes

and unique spirits still people it. Yet its genius remains:

the more it seems to stay the same, the more it also changes

Suddenly you see Oxford, a gray blur in the valley, as you drive over the hill from Newbury and the south. A haze of smoke, age, and legend veils her, a locomotive snorts in her railway sidings, and all around her lie the moist green hills of the Midlands, like open lettuce leaves. Visionary and beckoning stand her spires and domes, as Jude the Obscure glimpsed them long ago, for Oxford possesses always the quality of an idea.

She is more than a city, more than a railroad station, more than a road junction, more even than a university. She epitomizes a remarkable kingdom, here in the belly of England; she is a shrine to the truth, where many a fine soul has worshiped; she is a paradigm of the human conflict between the right and the wrong, the spiritual and the material, the ugly and the beautiful; and most of all she is an aspiration, a sad reminder of what the world might be—the turn of a phrase and the joy of a discovery and the smile of a pretty girl in a punt. Her comprehension transcends classes and races and grasps the whole range of human experience, from the sublime to the rock bottom. She has been fouled by time and degradation. She has been fortified by centuries of controversy, rivalry, and rancor. She stands beyond everyday logic, crooked, deep, and contradictory. She is not a large place—from your bump in the road you may see the whole of her, and inspect her suburbs in a sweep from Headington to Hinksey. But as an Englishman in America once observed, when asked which Oxford he came from, this is not Oxford, Missis-

sippi, nor Oxford, Nova Scotia, nor Oxford, New Zealand, nor even simply Oxford, England: this is Oxford, All the Bloody World.

The trappings of Oxford are hideous. Around her core of pinnacled beauty the modern suburbs lie faceless and blighted, genteel mock Tudor or heedless functional, endless housing estates in awful symmetry, cheap red brick and chromium plate, miles of mess and acres of apathy. On her eastern fringes sprawl the great car factories and steelworks of Cowley. On her southern flank a little wilderness of railroad tracks, gasometers, huts, and reservoirs stands like a drab no man's land beyond the canal. A pulsing, stifling stream of traffic clogs her ancient arteries, rattles her mullioned windows, and keeps her celebrated structures always shuddering.

For she lies in the very middle of England. Oxford was born, before the first universities were conceived, as the guardian of fords across the two rivers, Thames and Cherwell, which meet here and make this wide sedgy valley a place of vapors, water meadows, swans, and mottled lilies. Across this fulcrum the traffic of trade has passed since Saxon times, some by river, some by road: from London westward to Bristol, from Southampton and Winchester to the remote cities of the north. Bridges were built, with a protective fortress; guilds of merchants came into being; famous trading fairs were established. By the twelfth century this was one of the busiest and most prosperous of English cities, with a strong sense of community and a keen eye to the main chance—it had, as the historian

Of This World?

The High

J. R. Green has claimed, "five centuries of borough life before a student appeared in its streets." Romantic myth, speculating among the quadrangles, attributes the foundation of Oxford variously to the Trojans, to the Druids, to King Mempric, who lived a millennium before Christ, or to the indistinct Saint Frideswide, saved at this spot by divine intervention from being ravished on the banks of the Thames. In fact, though, the place was almost certainly founded not by saints, kings, or scholars but by hardheaded Saxon merchants, marketmen, and transport contractors, with their feet on the ground and their minds on their moneybags.

By the twelfth century the University had sprung fitfully into being, and for several hundred years imposed a severe academic autocracy upon the old city, reducing it, as Green observes, from a "busy prosperous borough . . . to a cluster of lodging-houses." Today the pendulum has swung again, and the supremacy of Town over Gown, of matter over mind, is forcibly reasserted. Some 100,000 citizens live in Oxford, but scarcely a tenth of them have any connection with the University, and today there are many people in the civic suburbs who hardly realize that the institution exists, except for its quaint buildings ("proper unhealthy they look to me") and its comical traditions ("like something out of the Middle Ages, that's what I always say").

The big Cowley factories cast their shadow across the flavor of the place. To their generous payrolls the workers have flocked from half of England, and any morning in Cornmarket, the city's central shopping street, you may see them in their myriads: plain but patently prosperous people, raw of accent and homely of manner, with a margin of spindly, greased youths lounging around the coffee shops and a nub of stolid, jolly, down-to-earth Midlands housewives carrying tins of cat food in shopping baskets. Many a shiny store has sprung up to serve them, overwhelming the old-school grocers, watchmakers, custom tailors, and booksellers who used to represent the commerce of the street. Many a tattered tabloid flutters past the libraries, and many a whiff of twenty-cent perfume lingers in the cloistered lanes. The common man has invaded Oxford again, and he comes to town in such numbers, with so much money to spend, that this has become one of the most cruelly congested cities in Europe.

Everywhere in the public streets there is relentless noisy movement. The wide bypasses that ring Oxford are never empty, never silent, and the apex of the place, the ancient crossroads called Carfax, is so inundated with converging traffic that at dusk the policemen assume refulgent white coats, and are illuminated by spotlights.

Stand for half an hour at the top of the High, one of the world's loveliest thoroughfares, and you may observe a cross section of England on the move, a mirror of her functions, a gauge of her activities. Here is a double-decked trailer of gleaming new cars, bound for Lagos or New Orleans. Here is a coach-load of tourists, goggle-eyed at tinted windows. Here is a consignment of steel rods, pounding down from Birmingham to Southampton Docks, and here is a glittering expense-account Rolls-Royce, whisking some padded London magnate from board room to boudoir. You can see by the names on the tailboards how crucial is this vortex to the motion of England: London and Bristol, Portsmouth and Plymouth, Sheffield and Chester and Newcastle-on-Tyne. Oxford is a hub, and her two old road-bridges are nozzles through which, like a reluctant dentifrice, the impetus of the Midlands must be squeezed.

In a way it feels historically right. The commercial life of Oxford is marked by a resilient consistency, so that we may recognize many of its patterns far back in the Middle Ages. The Freemen of the city still meet in council. The Sheriff of Oxford, once a year, still mounts his horse to impound the Commoners' cattle grazing on Port Meadow. And for a perfect image of the continuity of the place, you should visit Oxford during the annual Saint Giles Fair, successor to the great trade fairs of medieval England. The whole of St. Giles, the widest street in Oxford, is cluttered with its stalls, tents, roundabouts, and generators, the barking of its buskers and the popping of its air guns; and sauntering among its side shows you may catch the Oxford people off guard, all pretense discarded. There they stroll still, the immemorial characters of England, every type and degree of mortal, from the exquisite patrician to the sleaziest, grubbiest half-gypsy slut in carpet slippers, from the sheepish parson to the pinch-faced, leather-jerkined, weedy but raucous motorcycle lout—all old English archetypes, and direct descendants, every one, from predecessors of the distant past, when the Cotswold Hills farmers brought their wool on the hoof to Oxford market and the city thugs cherished so violent an antipathy to the academic aesthetes that not an inch between Carfax and St. Mary's, it was said, had not been at one time or another soaked in student blood.

For always, through any Oxford scene, there stalks the scholar. The skin of Oxford is pocked and scarred, but the heart of the place remains ineffably beautiful: and this is because for eight centuries the old market town has sheltered one of Europe's noblest universities. It is not the car factories, the bridges, or the crossroads that make this Oxford, All the Bloody World: it is *Universitas Oxoniensis*. Miraculously the charm and integrity of this institution has survived the battering of the years. The population of Oxford has doubled in this century, and increased twelvefold in the past two hundred years, so that when you reach this legendary place at last, your head awhirl with madrigals and aphorisms, all the horror of hasty growth greets you with a sneer. But poke about a bit, give it time, reserve your judgments, and restrain your resentment, and presently you will realize that Oxford's essential character has triumphantly survived it all. It does not show at first. Like Kyoto, like Florence perhaps, Oxford is a private kind of entity, and if you wish to understand the place, you must look over the wall.

Clean across the city, stretching away into the country, with playing fields and boathouses, running-tracks and laboratories, sprawls the University. No central campus gives rigidity to this puzzling organism, no plan, no uniformity, no rule or universal authority clamps it into docility. Oxford University is its own master—since

1919 the State has paid the piper handsomely, but it still dare not call the tune; and the University itself consists of some thirty autonomous colleges, each a corporation sanctified by Royal Charter, each a thing of individual character, method, and style. This means that the inner texture of Oxford is unbelievably rich and varied. A warren of venerable societies straddles Carfax and the High, each with its own mellow quadrangles, its lawns and fine old lodgings, its cherished cedars or beeches, its watchful porters' lodges, its old portraits glimpsed through leaded windows, its bell heard bland but insistent across the tumbled roof tops. Turn any corner in the center of Oxford, step down any side lane from the nightmare of the traffic, and you will discover some corner of seduction. Oxford does not flaunt her splendors, as Cambridge does, which is why the tourists, hastily canceling their hotel bookings, so often take one look at Carfax and hurry on to Stratford.

Nobody quite knows when this University was born, though only the most determined romantics now attribute its foundation to King Alfred. Some say it began as a group of monastic schools, some think its first students were scholars expelled from Paris in a wave of xenophobia in 1167. Certainly by the end of the twelfth century there was a guild of teachers in the city, loosely coalesced in a *Studium Generale* on the French model; and a century later there were probably about fifteen hundred Oxford students, living in lodgings, inns, and communal societies known as "halls." As early as 1214 the *Studium Generale* received the first of its charters, giving it immunity from lay jurisdiction; the people of Oxford then agreed to pay an annual symbolic tribute to the University authorities, and have been paying it ever since. The University grew explosively, often in controversy and sometimes in violence: there were riots against the papal legate, fights against the Jews, quarrels between northerners and southerners, constant bloody battles between Town and Gown. Through it all learning flourished. Roger Bacon, Duns Scotus, Wycliffe, Colet, More, and Erasmus were all Oxford men, and under the influence of the Schoolmen and the Renaissance scholars the University so strengthened its links with the Continent that it became accepted as one of the world's prime intellectual centers.

By the time of the Reformation Oxford had developed its system of independent colleges, to one of which every undergraduate must belong. A great deal has happened to Oxford since then: the English Civil War, when King Charles moved his court to Christ Church; the Anglican religious ferments of the nineteenth century, which gave birth to the Oxford Movement; the foundation of the women's colleges; two world wars; the English social revolution; the irresistible advance of science as a fit subject for scholarship. Nevertheless the university system today, with its jealously preserved college autonomies, would be easily recognizable to any wandering scholar out of the Restoration.

It is true that in recent years the University authorities, the central but amorphous governing body, have been impelled into a livelier role: the immense cost of new laboratories, in particular, is beyond the means of individual colleges. Nevertheless the Oxford colleges remain proudly, resolutely, sometimes rather absurdly individual. They have their own incomes, sometimes sizable, derived from land ownership, skillful investment, and endowments of diverse kinds.

They decide their own curricula, and need accept no academic edicts from the University itself. They appoint their own instructors and choose their own students, so that each college still has a distinctive style and type of its own, from the socially glittering (Christ Church or New College) to the academically daunting (Balliol or Magdalen). They have their own traditions, customs, ranks, and honorifics—Christ Church is presided over by a Dean, Magdalen by a President, All Souls by a Warden, Worcester by a Provost, St. Edmund Hall by a Principal, Pembroke by a Master, Lincoln by a Rector. They are often shamefully selfish, notably uninterested in each others' anxieties, and they are sometimes pitifully shortsighted, cheerfully yielding to the pressures of big business for the sake of a quick sale or a promising endowment. Some critics think the system outmoded and demand the centralization of authority, administrative and academic; but it is the survival of the colleges—their persistent complexity, their hauteur and their stubbornness—that has maintained the constancy of Oxford life and kept the place unique.

In the old Benedictine cottages of Worcester College, for instance, you may recognize the original lodging houses of medieval Oxford, narrow, gabled, mullioned places, with dark, narrow staircases and gimcrack chimneys. In St. Edmund Hall, with its delectable flower-fragrant quadrangle, you may wander through the very last of the old residential "halls." In the fifteenth-century Divinity Schools you may see reflected the growing power and prestige of the *Studium Generale,* and in Wolsey's magnificent Christ Church you may sense the new social consciousness of the University, supplementing its poor scholars and earnest clerics with dazzling noblemen, fops, and playboys. The Age of Reason is epitomized in Magdalen's lovely new buildings, set among the deer groves; the very essence of the Tractarian Movement infuses the Victorian red-brick of Keble; all the rising prestige of science gleams out of the new laboratories beside the University parks. Above all, everywhere, among the colorful barges and boathouses on the river, in the vaulted reading rooms of the Bodleian Library, among the aromatic splendors of Christ Church Hall, in the great Ashmolean Museum or the spanking Playhouse—above all you may sense, everywhere among these structures, the endless variety, the breadth of idiosyncrasy, the pride and the pragmatism that give this institution its special pungent character.

It is an old, gnarled, evocative thing, *Universitas Oxoniensis.* Its buildings are not usually spectacular, but are mostly gentle and kindly, from the delicate little quadrangle of Corpus Christi to the benign classical rotunda, portly but dignified, called the Radcliffe Camera. Its corridors echo the tread of a thousand great men: Erasmus or Sir Walter Raleigh, Gladstone or Sir Philip Sidney, Gibbon, Shelley, John Wesley, William Penn, Pitt, Swinburne, Lewis Carroll, Chatham and Lord North, Inigo Jones and Christopher Wren, Max Beerbohm, Peel, Hakluyt the geographer, Rhodes the imperialist, Foxe the martyrologist, Richard Burton the Arabist, Sydney Smith and Charles James Fox and John Galsworthy and T. E. Lawrence and De Quincey.

Some of Oxford's sons are more than merely legendary, and seem to be physically, or perhaps psychically, perpetuated, so that when the wind is right you may still hear Samuel Johnson's heavy tread

The Radcliffe Camera

lumbering into Pembroke, or catch an echo of Dr. Spooner's celebrated hymn announcement—"Kinkering Kongs Their Titles Take." In particular Oxford feeds upon the spirit of its great eccentrics. There was Dr. Frank Buckland of Corpus Christi, a nineteenth-century geologist, who used to claim that he had eaten his way through the entire animal kingdom and that the mole tasted nastiest of all (shown the heart of a French king preserved in a silver casket at Nuneham, outside Oxford, this remarkable gourmand, so legend says, at once seized the precious relic and before anyone could stop him, gobbled it eagerly up). There was the nonagenarian Dr. Routh, President of Magdalen, who so loathed the onslaughts of material progress that he flatly refused to recognize the invention of the railway and altogether declined to believe in the existence of the Oxford line. There was the reverend mathematician Charles Lutwidge Dodgson, whose cupboards at Christ Church burst with the performing bears, musical boxes, toy trains, and puppets of his peculiar alter ego, Lewis Carroll. There was Richard Whateley the logician, later Archbishop of Dublin, who taught his pack of mongrel dogs to climb trees in Christ Church meadows and dive from them into the river Cherwell. And in our own time there was Canon Claude Jenkins of Christ Church, one of the grandest of them all, with his muffler every day of the year, his wide old-school clerical hat, his equal aversion to cats and to matrimony, the appalling dust-thickened confusion of his house, and his celebrated tobacco, personally blended, which his *Times* obituary described as "exuding a fragrance unknown to the generality of smokers."

Any university is a spiritual pyramid, a thing of cumulative shades and evocations, and Oxford in particular possesses this quality of inheritance, as though the examples of the past contribute still to the curricula of the present, as the gramophone playing in the empty

Christ Church

with the times—half of it is usually miles behind, the other half grotesquely premature—but it is an institution of subtle, ill-defined influence, exerted often through what the British Army used to call "the old boy net," and sometimes so powerful that between the wars, for instance, there was caustically rumored to be a private telephone line from 10 Downing Street to All Souls. It is a bastion of the conviction that a man is a soul before a citizen, that his progress toward fulfillment is not governed by the state of society or the conditions of nations.

Today, in a period of British political and economic decline, Oxford turns out interesting men as vigorously as ever—not many of the world's universities could boast among their recent alumni, to pluck only a few names from a multitude, a dramatic critic of Kenneth Tynan's brilliance, a politician as distinguished as Sir Edward Boyle, an actor like Richard Burton, a poet like Dom Moraes, a theatre director like Tony Richardson,* a literary critic as profound as John Wain, a novelist as funny as Kingsley Amis. In 1961 the Nawab of Pataudi captained Oxford's cricket team, and Prince Harald of Norway stroked the Balliol boat.

It was Matthew Arnold who described Oxford as the "home of lost causes, and forsaken beliefs, and unpopular names, and impossible loyalties." It was James I of England who observed: "Were I not a King, I would be an Oxford man." This university represents the very antithesis of the Ad-Mass civilization. Its splendid libraries boast no electronic catalogues, but are stained with learning and scholarly delight. Its doorsteps are worn deep with age, and here and there among the colleges you may stumble across a remnant of the city ramparts, long since integrated into academic life and looking so shaggy, pebbly, and eroded that it seems less like a wall than a geological formation. The clocks of the University move with ancient whirrs and ticks, and the doors of the University open with creaks and wheezes, and the gardens of the University, with their sensual abundance of design, their treasured creepers and their pampered lawns—the gardens of Oxford, for all their conceits and elaborations, seem inevitable and immemorial, as though they have sprung ready-clipped and weeded from the spongy subsoil of the Thames marshes.

Most of all, perhaps, it is the gardens that keep the heart of Oxford, for all the ravages of time and progress, still a place of breathtaking allure. One of the classic English experiences is to stand in the gardens of Merton College, say, on an afternoon of high summer, when the valley air hangs warm and heavy and the trees preside over a heavenly shade. The thud and roar of the traffic is only a suggestion beyond the college gateway. The four golden weather vanes of the chapel tower loiter above you in idle parallel. Before you Christ Church meadows lie damp and tufty, like a slab of open country, and away to the east the famous tower of Magdalen stands sentinel above its bridge. Merrily on the afternoon air hang the sounds of the river beyond the trees—the shouts of a rowing coach, a ripple of badinage, a girl's laughter, a snatch of song. From the shadowy staircases behind you emanate suggestions of donnish activity—a slow rustle of pages, the clink of a glass, arguments testily exchanged, the hint of a snore. The bumblebees potter benevolently

house can infuse some charm into the very attic rafters. Oxford still warms, in her crannies and her instincts, to the presence of the great Benjamin Jowett, Master of Balliol, of whom it was written:

> I come first. My name is Jowett:
> There's no knowledge but I know it.
> I am the Master of this College:
> What I don't know—isn't knowledge.

He was a little, fresh-faced man, fragile and taciturn, but he made Balliol a power in the world, and his fastidious, quirky integrity— "Never retract, never explain. Get it done and let them howl"—has left its permanent impression upon the Oxford ethos. In this university you can never quite evade the image of Keble, that inspired Tractarian fundamentalist ("When God made the stones, he made the fossils in them"), or Newman of the Oxford Movement, of whom it was said that he was perpetually "skimming along the verge of a logical catastrophe," or indeed Frank Buchman of the Oxford Group, with his smart young apostates and his publicist's faith, "world-changing through life-changing."

Oxford University is a place of ever-eddying controversy, from the old altercations of the Schoolmen to the recent donnish differences concerning the necessity of the war against Hitler. In the sour days before the war the Oxford Union voted that it would "in no circumstances fight for its King and country," and today Oxford still seethes with young outrage, from the impassioned protests of the nuclear disarmers, marching beneath Bertrand Russell's escutcheon, to the baroque flamboyances of the irrepressible Tories, still entrenched behind champagne crates and debutante invitations in the elegant Peckwater rooms. The University is seldom in step

*See "Revolt Against the West End," by Irving Wardle, on page 26.

from blossom to blossom. A lawn mower is busy beyond the wall. Somebody is knocking a ball about with a cricket bat, to the magical hollow thud of well-oiled wood on leather. There is a smell of cut grass, books, old wood, flowers, linseed oil, and stone. There is a soft rustle of leaves, and a squeak from the weather vanes above, when a breeze whispers off the river.

Some will call it an outmoded world that these sensations represent. Some will call it doomed anyway, as Oxford reluctantly tacks to the winds of time. But for some it is a glimpse of the world as it might have been, of England as her lovers used to see her, before disillusionment set in. For Town or Gown, divine or unspeakable, old or new, vital or fuddy-duddy—whichever face she presents, Oxford is always a mirror of England. She draws her inspiration from the genius of the nation, and all her faults and virtues, all her scars and pleasures, are but microcosms of a greater model. Hundreds of thousands of foreigners have lived in Oxford down the centuries, contributing marvelously to her glories, and there are always hundreds of foreigners about today, from eminent visiting professors to the blonde German girls with bicycles and airline bags who have come to help with the children and learn the language. Yet no city in England remains more English, and no institution remains more faithful to its origins than this remarkable University.

In Oxford you may encounter the whole range of the English species, *homo anglicus,* from the highest type of civilized and sagacious animal to the lowest humped and furtive degenerate. At any one moment you may find here twenty or thirty of the cleverest men in England, ten or twelve of the most distinguished, half a dozen who have become nationally famous as television performers or writers of detective novels; but you may also bump into as primitive a type of urbanized peasant as survives anywhere in Western Europe. The climate of Oxford is dank, and the Oxfordshire native often has

mold in his soul. There is eccentricity in the air of the place, and bloody-mindedness, the defiance of swart bucolics, the supreme indifference of dons. Nowhere in Oxford is altogether prosaic. Even the drab old railway station has its own glamour—did not Zuleika Dobson arrive there on the train from Paddington? Even the grubby Trill Mill stream, emerging sluggishly into daylight from its subterranean channels—even that gloomy waterway has romance, for did not Lawrence of Arabia once sail down it in a punt? In Christ Church meadows Dr. Johnson slid on the ice. In Alice's Shop in Saint Aldate's the White Queen turned into the old sheep knitting behind her counter.

You may find Oxford disappointing at first, as Hilaire Belloc's stranger did:

> *Is it from here the people come,*
> *Who talk so loud, and roll their eyes,*
> *And stammer? How extremely odd!*
> *How curious! What a great surprise!*

You may not sense her enchantment from your first sniff on the Newbury road, your first glimpse of her gasworks and musty tobacconists. Give her a week or two, though, and her old slow magic will enthrall you too, as it has generations of addicts before you. She is no paragon, no virgin Paradise, no Shangri-La. She is beloved, by the truest of her admirers, in a special, wry kind of way: because she is beautiful but blotched, wise but always fallible, noble but tainted, proud but pitiful: because she remains, more than most cities in a steely world, incurably, hopelessly, heart-rendingly human.

This is the second in a group of essays on certain key centers and cities by Mr. Morris, roving correspondent of the Manchester Guardian *and author of many books. His essay on Delhi appeared in the May, 1962,* HORIZON; *the next, on Venice, will appear in March of this year.*

The Clarendon and Sheldonian Buildings.

ILLUSTRATED FOR HORIZON BY JOHN GLASHAN

Far removed from Broadway, an adventurous husband and
wife are producing surprising new images in the theatre

A Pair of Modern Masquers

The town of Pineville in the scenic hill country of southeastern Kentucky is not celebrated as a center of the performing arts. Yet every summer since 1959 its Pine Mountain State Park has harbored an extraordinary production created by a husband-and-wife team of young college teachers, who have also taken their work to audiences up and down the land and to European capitals as well. Entitled simply *The Book of Job*, it is a highly stylized enactment of the Old Testament chronicle—a masque in which the performers wear make-up and costumes that transform them into Byzantine mosaics in slow motion, assembling in stately groups and walking and wheeling with ecclesiastical dignity as they speak the words of the King James Bible.

Orlin Corey was a professor of speech and drama at Georgetown College, Kentucky, when he adapted the text into a series of monologues, dialogues, and choruses, and directed student players in the roles. His wife, Irene, was teaching stage design when she costumed and designed the whole production in a manner that has set a unique mark upon it. To accomplish the mosaic effects (see opposite) she pasted scraps of material of many colors to the robes and headgear of the players; then she applied formal mosaic patterns to their faces and hands, first drawing a network of lines to represent the lead strips of a stained-glass window, then filling in the spaces between with varicolored paint.

Reared in the upland, the Coreys' version of the Book of Job attracted international attention when it was performed at the Brussels World's Fair, since which time it has toured England, played to packed pews in New York City's Christ Church Methodist, and been seen in theatres from Williamstown, Massachusetts, to Miami, Florida. A leading authority on religious drama in English, E. Martin Browne, has said of it that "the décor, script, and production are

Orlin and Irene Corey

of exceptional power"; and the size and range of its audiences seem to confirm this judgment.

But the Coreys have not been content to rest on the laurels of their *Job* (so different in conception from Archibald MacLeish's recent dramatic gloss on the story, *J.B.*, yet apparently hardly less durable than it). Moving on from Kentucky to Shreveport, Louisiana, where since 1960 they have been in charge of the Department of Speech and Drama at Centenary College, they have extended their field. At Shreveport they have organized a students' drama group, The Jongleurs, dedicated to experimental productions. Unlike the original jongleur, that minstrel-errant of the Middle Ages, the Coreys have at their disposal a handsome theatre, the Marjorie Lyons Playhouse; like the jongleur, they may take to the road at any time to carry

their art to far places. Among their most striking Louisiana productions is another highly stylized enactment—the fable *Reynard the Fox* as dramatized by the Belgian playwright Arthur Fauquez, and marked in their hands by extraordinary costume and make-up effects (overleaf).

Recently the Coreys have also mounted many other plays after their own fashion, for dissemination from Shreveport. In November, 1961, they staged Arthur Miller's *The Crucible*, with its meaningful account of bigotry as embodied in the witch-hunt trials of seventeenth-century Massachusetts—an appropriate play for Orlin Corey to have directed, since he himself, of New England stock, is a descendant, nine times removed, of that historic Giles Corey of Salem who was crushed to death for speaking out against the trials, and whose last words, echoed in the play, were, "More weight!" Some citizens of Shreveport took umbrage at the Miller play, but Corey defended it as "a fearful memory of the American conscience."

Ever individual in their choices and ideas of production, the Coreys have also brought to Shreveport their staging of Shakespeare's neglected tragicomedy, *The Winter's Tale;* Shaw's satire about the Salvation Army, *Major Barbara;* Norman Corwin's adaptation of the 1858 debates between Abraham Lincoln and Stephen A. Douglas, *The Rivalry;* Molière's sardonic comedy, *The Miser;* and a trio of religious plays from Britain: T. S. Eliot's *Murder in the Cathedral,* P. W. Turner's *Cry Dawn in Dark Babylon,* and Christopher Fry's *A Sleep of Prisoners.* Last summer the Coreys and their Jongleur troupe also entered the musical-play lists with an all-singing, all-dancing satire on international conferences, entitled *The Peace Gimmick*—a long dramatic distance from their solemnly masked *Job,* but again testimony to theatrical originality far removed from Broadway.

Wearing costume and make-up designed by Irene Corey to suggest Byzantine mosaics, actor Warren Hammack appears in the title role of The Book of Job, *Orlin Corey's masque-like adaptation of the King James Bible text.*

89

From the Bible

PHOTOGRAPHS JERRY MITCHELL

Orlin Corey as Time in The Winter's Tale

... to the Fable

The cast of the Coreys' Book of Job

Reynard the Fox (Randolph Tallman)

After their Book of Job, *Orlin and Irene Corey embarked on an equally ambitious production, that of* Reynard the Fox *by the Belgian playwright Arthur Fauquez, who writes in the fabulist tradition of Aesop and Jean de La Fontaine. For this animal tale set in a forest in medieval Europe, Irene Corey demonstrated again that costume and make-up can be a single design element, and so add visual force to verbal drama, much as masks and cosmetics did in the ancient Greek theatre, in Oriental plays, and in the commedia dell'arte of 17th-century Italy. To simulate the faces of the animals, she painted across the actors' features, creating "flexible masks," part human, part beast, which allowed them to grimace and smile. The cast went to a zoo to study the porcupine's rolling walk, the swift, nervous movements of the fox, and the bear's stumble. So convincing were the imitations that one bemused member of the audience asked, "Wherever did you find that giant porcupine?"*

in the Corey Theatre

Brun the Bear (Hal Proske)

Epinard the Porcupine (Bob Harmon)

Tiecelin the Crow (Ruthanne Cozine)

Lendore the Marmot (Sylvia Cardwell)

Ysengrin the Wolf (John Broadus)

By W. H. ARMSTRONG

MR. ELIOT REVISITS THE WASTE LAND

Two leading experts on waste lands are T. S. Eliot of St. Louis, Harvard, and then London, who wrote memorably of one long ago, and the lawyer Newton Minow of Chicago and then Washington, D.C., where as chairman of the Federal Communications Commission he supervises what he has identified as another. Suppose that poet Eliot were confronted by an American television set, as Commissioner Minow often is in his line of duty: What might he have to say then? While awaiting his reaction, some words are put in his mouth by an American with an ear to Eliot and a close eye on television—a particularly close eye, since W. H. Armstrong, a TV executive, is now News Director of station WRAL at Raleigh, North Carolina.

April is the cruelest month, breeding
Cowboys out of the dead land, mixing
Reruns and pilot films, stirring
Tonight Show with Today.
Winter kept us warm, covering
Sullivan with Walt Disney, feeding
Lawrence Welk with Mister Ed.
Summer surprised us, coming over the coaxial
With a shower of Talent Scouts; we stopped on Mitch Miller,
And went on to midnight, into the Paargarten,
And drank coffee, and watched for an hour.

And when we were children, staying at Grandma's,
My cousin, he showed me Yogi Bear
And I was frightened. He said, Marie,
Marie, hold on tight. And down we went
With Captain Kangaroo, there you feel free.
I look, much of the night, and go to bed in the morning.

Where is the Ripcord one pulls, what M Squad grows
Out of this Prime Time? O Viewer,
You cannot say, or guess, for you know only
A heap of unpicked options, where the ratings frown,
And the sponsors give no shelter, the critics no relief,
And the Avails no sign of comfort. Only
There is a glow from this bright tube
(Come in under the glow of this bright tube),
And I will show you something different from either
Bill Cullen at morning grinning before you
Or Wagon Train at evening rolling to meet you;
I will show you lust in a canful of beer.

They gave us Dick Van Dyke first two years ago;
They called it Situation Comedy.
—Yet, when we came back, late, from Price is Right,
Your arms full and your eyes wet, I could not
Speak and my eyes failed, I was neither
Happy nor sad, and I knew all,
Viewing into the magic screen, the beauty
Of love and hope and life and booty.

Madame Arlene, famous *bonne vivante*
Has a good heart, nevertheless
Is known to be the sharpest woman in TV
With a wicked stock of ad libs. Here, said she,
Is your destiny, the drowned Red Buttons,
(Those are Zoomars that were his eyes. Look!)
Here is La Kilgallen, the Lady of the Knocks,
The lady of guesstimations.
Here is the man of Cheyenne, and here the Horse,
And here is the game-legged deputy, and this gun,
Which has blanks, is something he carries on his hip,
Which I am privileged to see. I seldom find
The Hanged Man (strung up). Fear death by lead.
I see crowds of dancers, springing from the wings.
Thank you. If you see dear Miss Donna,
Tell her I must bring her renewal myself:
One must be so circumspect these days.

You who were with Mason at the bar in court!
The acquittal you planted last year in your garden,
Has it begun to bloom? Will it be resurrected this summer?
Or has the sudden Minowpause disturbed its bed?
Keep the Watchdog far hence, no friend of men,
Or with his pick he'll dig it up again!
And Fall will bring us Tall Man . . . and then?

Hurry up, come on please, it's time
Please hurry up, come on, it's time
Goodnight Bill. Goodnight Jack. Goodnight Jill.
      Goodnight.
Goodnight sweet, good ladies, Hazel is triumphant yet.
Goodnight David.
Goodnight Chet.

After the black-gray light on sweaty faces
After the reddened eyes in the parlor
After the agony that is Casey's
The glower that his patient faces;
Penthouse and prairie and reverberation
Of Sunset Strip over distant Flintstones

They who were firmed up are now slack
We who were bright-eyed are now blind
On the other channel.

Camera no longer candid, and the limp residuals
Waited for rain, while the black clouds
Gathered far distant, over Madison Avenue.
Kildare crouched, humped in between station ID's.
Then spoke the thunder.
DA
Datta Datta Dot Dot.
Da-da-da dot dot.*

What have we given:
My friend, a worn resistor
The flip-flop of a rolling picture
Which an age of transience can never recover.
By this, and this only, we have existed
Which is more smoke and less enjoyment
A jadedness that grrrrips the road
Or in moments draped by the beneficent Downs
Or under dreams, restless in the Twilight Zone
In our empty rooms.

                I sat upon the couch
Switching, with Sea Hunt before me
Shall I at least gather my Bonanzas?
Surfside Six is falling down
Falling down
Father no longer knows best
No room for Daddy
Less for a hundred Cains
Willing but unable
To Play my Hunch

Then?
Da
Datta Datta Dot Dot
Da-da-da dot dot.

Fade to black.

*Chant to the cadence of the Maxwell House Ballad.

Pascal

He had one of the best minds of all time, but it was at war with itself. One half

of it he gave to God; with the other he laid the foundations of the Age of Reason

Blaise Pascal lived a scant thirty-nine years,
but if one is a prodigy, as he was,
that is time enough to earn immortality. At
nineteen he invented his pascaline,
the first real calculating machine (opposite).
Although it won him early fame (but
little money), he is remembered today chiefly
for his later scientific discoveries,
Pascal's Law, and two books: the Provincial
Letters *and the* Pensées. *His greatest*
celebrity did not come until after he died,
in 1662; except for one quick sketch
from life, all his portraits—including the one
from which this engraving was made—
are posthumous and based on his death mask.

By MORRIS BISHOP   *Photographs by* ERICH LESSING

On the slopes of the Puy de Dôme, above his native Clermont-Ferrand, a tube of mercury recalls the experiment by which Pascal proved that air has weight. He had his brother-in-law carry two such tubes up the mountain. As they ascended into the thinner atmosphere, the column of mercury fell in the tube; it rose again on the descent into the valley. Aside from the larger implications of this discovery, it gave us the barometer. Pascal was twenty-five at the time, and had not yet undergone the spiritual crisis that eventually caused him to seek the austere solitude of a cell at the convent of Port-Royal des Champs (at right).

Every now and then humanity produces an intellectual sport, a genius, a mental monster. We expect the great mind to serve us, and so, usually, it does. But with its higher order of values it is likely to dismiss our own and to perceive and pursue aims that astonish our earthliness. Thus Isaac Newton abandoned science to spend his incomparable mind on unriddling the prophecies of Daniel. Thus Joseph Priestley, the discoverer of oxygen, came to America and settled in frontier Pennsylvania, to write twenty-five volumes of unreadable, or at least unread, theology. Thus also Blaise Pascal.

What made the great mind? The genes, of course, or if you prefer, God. But notice Pascal's background and development. He was born in Clermont-Ferrand, in the center of France, in 1623. His mother died when he was three. His father, a civil servant and amateur scientist, recognized that he had fathered a prodigy and resigned his post to devote himself entirely to the education of Blaise and his two remarkable sisters. The father's views were unorthodox. He believed that the need of knowledge must precede knowledge, that reason and judgment must precede formal study. He taught the experimental method: observe, classify, generalize. Thus Blaise, at eleven, noticed that a china dish struck with a knife hums until silenced by a touch of the hand. "Why?" he said, like any child. Unlike any child, he found the answers unsatisfactory and made a series of experiments on sound and wrote a treatise much applauded by his elders. Having been kept in ignorance of geometry, he invented, at twelve, his own, and was discovered doing his version of Euclid's thirty-second proposition on the kitchen floor. At sixteen he printed some remarks on conic sections that herald our projective geometry.

Thus he was trained to originality, to genius. He never knew the orthodoxies and subjections of a school, nor the group spirit and rivalries of a school; he was destined for lonely apartness. Nor did he ever play, or build his body in sports and games. Nature shook her head and sighed.

When Blaise was sixteen his father was appointed collector of internal revenue in Rouen. The post was an exacting one; Blaise was drafted to aid in the endless calculations. Promptly bored by drudgery, he wondered if the mechanical work could not be done by a machine. Characteristically, he proceeded from the problem to its practical solution. He created the first calculating machine.

His initial, momentous idea was to conceive the digits of a number as arranged in wheels; each wheel, after making a complete revolution, should turn its left-hand neighbor a fraction of a revolution. (Look at your speedometer.)

One machine preserved in the Paris Musée des Arts et Métiers is a polished brass box, about fourteen by five by three inches (see page 95). On the top, or working surface, we see a row of eight movable dials. The right-hand dial, twelve-slotted, represents deniers, or pence; the next dial, twenty-slotted, represents sous, or shillings; the remainder, ten-slotted, are for livres, or pounds. At the back of the box is a series of windows in which numbers, on drums, appear.

The dials are actuated by a stylus. To perform a simple addition, for example 9 pounds 6 shillings and sevenpence plus 10 pounds 15 shillings and eightpence, one begins at the right, inserts the stylus in the seventh slot, and revolves

*Determined to stamp out Jansenism, Louis XIV
forcibly removed the nuns from Port-
Royal des Champs in 1709 and razed it the following year. Today nothing is left
of the convent where Pascal wrote his* Pensées
*but the farm buildings and a well-
windlass he is thought to have designed. By
a simple set of reduction gears it
raises a barrel of water weighing 270 pounds
while an empty barrel descends.*

the wheel clockwise, like a telephone dial, to the stop which catches the stylus. The proper figures appear in the windows. Begin again with the second sum. We read the total in the windows: 20 pounds 2 shillings and threepence. To subtract: push back the brass strip at the back of the box, disclosing a second set of windows. Dial the minuend and the subtrahend; the remainder appears in the windows. Multiplication and division (which are only abridged additions and subtractions) take longer.

It was an extraordinary mechanical achievement. "Pascal knew how to animate copper and give wit to brass," said an admiring friend. Pascal made at least fifty machines and built on them great hopes of gain. But the *pascaline* did not sell. Since accurate gear-cutting was impossible, the mechanism was forever getting out of order, and only Pascal or one of his workmen could fix it. And it was too expensive. Though it could do the work of half a dozen men, the half-dozen men were still cheaper than the machine. Technology had to wait for economics to catch up.

In mathematics Pascal's work is known to every professional. He created the theory of probability, gave Leibniz the hint that became his infinitesimal calculus, and—as a diversion from a toothache—solved the problem of the cycloid. Most of his mathematical work is too technical for exposition here. But physics, or the world we live in, is everybody's business. We are all physicists, or we would be dead.

In Pascal's time there was much learned talk of the vacuum, or the void, which was identified by verbal habit with *nihil*, nothing. Philosophers argued that nature abhors a vacuum, that a Nothing cannot be a Something. But Pascal was impressed by reports of Torricelli's famous experiment, today a high-school commonplace. A forty-inch glass tube is filled with mercury, then turned smartly upside down, with the open end in a bowl of mercury. The mercury in the tube sinks to a height of about thirty inches, leaving a ten-inch gap at the sealed top of the tube. What is in the gap and how does it get there? Pascal concluded that it is a real vacuum, that the weight of mercury in the tube balances the weight of air on the mercury in the bowl. He developed his thesis with a sensational series of experiments. He had, for instance, forty-six-foot glass tubes made, a triumph of glass

*After Pascal's sister Jacqueline entered the
convent of Port-Royal de Paris (left)
in 1652, he himself was increasingly drawn toward the monastic life. But these
were the years of his greatest worldly success,
when all the learned men of Europe
followed his discoveries in pure mathematics
and his experiments in physics. At
that time there was no such thing as standard-
ized measurements or laboratory methods. Pascal designed his own equipment, and
with the help of the glass blowers
of Rouen created the precise and elegant instruments shown opposite. But in
1654 he virtually abandoned science for the
examination of man's relation to God.*

blowing. He bound them to ships' masts, pivoted in the middle. He filled the tubes with water, wine, or oil, reversed
them so that the open ends sat in tubs of liquid, removed
the stoppers, and saw the fluids fall and create measurable
vacuums.

If air has weight, he argued, there should be less at the
top of a mountain than at its foot; hence the measure of
mercury in a Torricellian tube should vary with the alti-
tude. The Puy de Dôme stands conveniently four thousand
feet above his native city of Clermont. He commissioned
his brother-in-law, Florin Périer, to make the great experiment. Two Torricellian tubes were borne by a party of en-
thusiastic amateurs to the summit. The mercury dropped
about three inches, and rose again on the return journey.
Meanwhile control tubes set up in the city had remained
unchanged. Thus the weight of air was not only demonstrated but measured. And thus Pascal propounded the
principle of the aneroid barometer.

Pascal continued with important work on hydrostatics,
or the equilibrium and pressure of liquids. He enunciated
the general rule of the transmission of pressure in fluids,
now known as Pascal's law. He proposed the hydraulic
press. He stated, apparently for the first time, the principle
of the elasticity of gases. He tried to relate the behavior of
fluids and gases in corresponding formulas. And he wrote
some precious analyses of scientific method and of the
scientific mind.

But science palled. He wrote: "I had passed a long time
in the study of the abstract sciences; and the limited number
with whom one can treat thereof had disgusted me with
them. When I began the study of man I saw that these abstract sciences are not proper to man and that I was stray-
ing farther from my natural state in penetrating them than
others were in their ignorance of them, but I thought at
least to find many companions in the study of man, and
that this was the true study proper to him. I was mistaken;
there are still fewer who study man than geometry."

He plunged into the study of man in society, or social
psychology, with a scientist's thoroughness. He had his
entree at court, in literary salons, in the high bourgeoisie of
Paris. He attended the theatre, and gambled like a gentleman. Did he know love? Very likely; but if so, most of the
evidence was carefully suppressed after his death.

His father died; his beloved sister Jacqueline became a
nun at Port-Royal; his married sister Gilberte was far away
in Clermont. He was alone, sick, wretched. Science and man
had failed him. He turned to God.

His God was the God of Jansenism. This was a movement within the Catholic Church, proposing a rigorous,
fundamentalist interpretation of sacred texts and of the
early Fathers. Its doctrine was grim, dwelling all on man's
guilt, from which he can be redeemed only by God's rare
predestined grace. The chief enemies of the Jansenists were
the Jesuits, who had developed a more modernist theology,
more kindly toward errant man.

The headquarters of Jansenism were the convents of Port-
Royal de Paris and Port-Royal des Champs. The Paris convent is now the Hôpital de la Maternité, on the Boulevard
de Port-Royal. The nuns' choir has become a laundry, and

When Pascal's body was laid out for burial, two discoveries were made:
that he wore next his skin a spiked wire belt to mortify
the flesh, and that sewn into the lining of his coat was the record
of a great mystical experience. On a sheet of paper
dated November 23, 1654, he had written, in part: "From about half
past ten in the evening until about half past twelve,
FIRE. Certitude, certitude, feeling, joy, peace. . . . Joy, joy, joy,
tears of joy. . . . Jesus Christ. I have been separated
from him; I have fled him, renounced him, crucified him. Let me never
be separated from him. . . . Renunciation, total and sweet."

in the cells consecrated to virginity the poor women of Paris suffer the pains of childbirth. Port-Royal des Champs stood fifteen miles southwest of Paris, in the lovely valley of the Chevreuse. It was razed by angry old Louis XIV in 1710; it is now marked only by a votive museum and by the farm buildings, Les Granges. About the two Port-Royals clustered a group of adherents, the *solitaires*, mostly men of distinction fleeing the void of their world, seeking to fill the vacuum in their hearts. They devoted themselves to the meanest of labors in the service of the nuns, their Ladies.

To this center Pascal turned, in disgust with the world. And on the evening of November 23, 1654, from half past ten to half past twelve, God came in fire to give him a mystic revelation. This was the capital experience of Pascal's life. His record of that fiery vision, of the coming of certitude, joy, peace, and grace, he wrote on a sheet of paper, which is now one of the treasures of the Bibliothèque Nationale (see page 103). We call it his Memorial, for during the rest of his life he carried it always with him, sewed in the lining of his coat. It was discovered only when his body was laid out for burial.

Was it God who spoke to him? Or was he victim of a hallucination? Abnormal psychology can give of his experience a description that has no need of God. But abnormal psychology can never prove anything to a mystic. He smiles, and says: "I was there. I know."

After his night of fire Pascal abandoned the world and science to devote himself to the care of his soul. "What would you say of a leper who, indifferent to his gnawing disease, would talk of botany or astronomy to his doctor?" He made long retreats at Port-Royal des Champs, living with the solitaries at the Granges, doing his own housework, delighting in the earthen dish and wooden spoon which, his sister in religion told him, are the gold and precious stones of Christianity. He is said to have designed, during one of his visits, the well-windlass, still in operation (see pages 98–99). The ascription of the device to Pascal rests only on an old tradition first recorded in 1723, but there is nothing unlikely about it. His habit was always to pass from the recognition of a need to its satisfaction. Visiting Port-Royal's Little Schools, he was annoyed by the illogicality of the traditional system of teaching reading. He devised a new method, that which became standard throughout the Western world. And even in little things: irritated by waiting for sedan-chair bearers, the taxis of the time, he established in Paris the first omnibus company. Annoyed at fishing for his watch, he amazed his friends by strapping it to his wrist.

Jansenism was under attack in those days, and Pascal was summoned to aid its defense. He did so in his *Provincial Letters*, a series of polemics addressed to the general public. These turned from defense to offense, to a savage attack on Jesuit theology and practice, particularly on casuistry and on the relaxation of moral principle by comforting concessions to man's weakness. To reach the large public Pascal found an easy, colloquial style, based on speech, which determined the form of French prose even to our own time. The effect of the *Provincial Letters* on Western man's common fund of ideas has been immense. They seem to render theology so clear and easy that every man felt himself competent to argue with the doctors. They broadcast the legend of Jesuit duplicity for all the world to read. The weapon forged against the Jesuits fell into the hands of Catholicism's enemies, and soon into those of Christianity's enemies. Read as they are in every French school, they still provide knowing pupils with anticlerical arguments and examples, remembered their lives long. What a fate for Pascal, the champion of Catholic faith!

The *Provincial Letters* angered rather than convinced the high churchmen. The pope condemned Jansenist theology and forbade the order to propagandize or to recruit new members. Pascal then turned to a new and greater task—the defense of the Christian doctrine by purely rational means, an Apology for Christianity.

As his health steadily grew worse he could no longer trust his clouding memory. "Escaped thought, I wished to write it; I write instead that it escaped me." He jotted down his thoughts as they came to him, now in an illegible invalid's scribble, now in a clear, confident hand. When too weak to write he would dictate the scheme of an idea or a few happy phrases. He would return from church with a suggestion scratched on his fingernails with a pin.

These notes are the *Pensées* of Pascal, as we possess them today. Some are incomprehensible; some are commonplace memoranda; some are fragments of dialogue, imaginary conversations with objectors; some are careful developments, pages long; some are lyric outbursts, forever memorable and unforgotten. The *Pensées* make one of the great books of

French literature, of all literature. They are admitted to every Five-foot Shelf, to every collection of Great Books. They are the comfort of soldiers, the companions of exiles, night voices to fevered men, songs in solitary hearts.

One can construct from the *Pensées* the general scheme of his unwritten *Apology for Christianity*. Let me string together some of his thoughts on a connecting thread:

Look first at the natural state of man. What is man in nature? A nullity in relation to infinity, an all in relation to nullity, a mid-point between nothing and everything. . . . Forever uncertain and drifting, we sail on a vast middle sea, impelled from one shore to another. To whatever fixed point we think to tie and cling, it quakes and fails us; and if we follow it, it escapes our clutch, slips away and flees us in eternal flight. Nothing stops for us. This is the state which is natural to us, and yet the most unwelcome to us; we burn with the desire to find a firm footing, a last constant base whereon to build a tower rising to infinity; but all our foundation cracks, and the earth opens, down to the abyss. . . . "The eternal silence of infinite space terrifies me."

Man is worse than weak, ignorant, and vain; he is evil. His actions are determined by self-interest, a marvelous instrument for putting out our own eyes agreeably. We would do anything for the applause we love. We even lose our life joyfully, if only people will talk about it. We hate the truth and those who tell it to us; we are only disguise, falsehood, and hypocrisy. All men naturally hate each other. What a sink is the heart of man, how full of ordure!

But look more closely; something noble peers from the eyes of that ogreish face. The creature thinks; he is not utterly a stone or a brute. Visibly he is made to think; that is all his dignity and his merit. Man is only a reed, the weakest in nature; but he is a thinking reed. There is no need that the whole universe arm itself to crush him; a vapor, a drop of water, is enough to kill him. But even if the universe should crush him, man would still be nobler than that which kills him, because he knows he dies; and of the advantage the universe has over him the universe knows not at all. By thought man has learned the truth; by it he conceives a possible nobility. He knows himself to be wretched; a tree, a ruined house, does not know itself to be wretched. Man's very wretchedness proves his grandeur, for his are the woes of a great lord, a king unthroned.

This is man—part misery, part grandeur—two opposites which cannot be resolved. What a monster is man, judge of all things, witless worm; casket of truth, sewer of incertitude and error; glory and refuse of the universe!

Of man's duality God has given us a lucid and convincing explanation. Man was once perfect and has become corrupt through sin. His misery is natural to his present condition; his grandeur indicates his lost perfection.

Christianity offers a means of rescue from this parlous state. A sensible man will test the proposition that the Christian God exists. You could bet on that proposition. If you bet that God exists, and win, you win everything; if you lose, you lose nothing.

You will examine the overwhelming proofs of Christianity's truth, the miracles, the fulfillment of prophecies, the persistence of the faith. But in the end you will have no need of proofs based on fallible human reason. The heart has its reasons that reason does not know. It is by the heart that we know the first principles, and reason must rest on the perceptions of the heart and of instinct. There is nothing so conformant to reason as the disavowal of reason. Christianity, so rich in proofs, miracles, witnesses, signs and wisdom, dismisses them all and declares to you that none of these can change us and make us capable of knowing and loving God, but only the virtue of the folly of the cross, without wisdom and signs.

Thus in the end Pascal surrenders all his proofs, to rest on man's need to love his God.

As Pascal meditated and wrote, his health continued to fail. Modern diagnoses are insecure, but there is some agreement on peritoneal tuberculosis, accompanied by an evil growth in the brain. He was tortured by frightful headaches, but he blessed God for his sufferings, regarding them as a fire burning away his sins little by little by a daily sacrifice. Sickness, he said, is the natural state of Christians.

He hurried the end of his sufferings by austerities. He refused any concession to appetite. He made secretly a wire belt, with sharp points turning inward against the flesh, and when he felt any stirring of pleasure or vanity he would rub his elbows against it, to wound his spirit through the body. He tortured also his sisters, forbidding any show of affection toward him, forbidding even Gilberte's children to embrace their mother: "Jesus shakes off his disciples to enter his agony. We must shake off our nearest and dearest to imitate him."

He died three hundred years ago last August, aged thirty-nine. The direct cause was a hemorrhage of the brain. The great mind was poisoned by the corruption of the blood, the corruption of life.

He was as authentic a genius as our world has produced. But the logic of genius would not permit him to rest satisfied with the reasonable work of genius, the service of human knowledge. He was trying, by force of will, to pass from what he called the order of minds to the higher order of charity. He was attempting sainthood, attempting to take the heavenly city by storm. He tried to surpass and abandon humanity; he succeeded only, in pain and misery, in abandoning himself. We commonplace men and women, content with our humanity, must regard him with wonder and pity, recognizing in him a victim of the curse of genius.

Morris Bishop is a teacher (Cornell), a translator (Eight Plays of Molière), a biographer (Ronsard, Pascal, La Rochefoucauld), and a writer of light verse (A Bowl of Bishop).

ON THE HORIZON

DRAWINGS BY NICHOLAS SOLOVIOFF

Is the great American public becoming altogether too friendly to contemporary artists and writers, and is there a clear and present danger of a love affair between Philistines and anti-Philistines that may raise the question of who has seduced whom?

Murray Kempton, in his cautionary "The Artist in Our Time" on page 73 of this issue, views the situation with alarm, feeling that what he regards as the public's increasing and uncritical acceptance of whatever's new in the arts suggests not so much that the public has been had, as that it is the artist who has been tamed, the rebel who has been made respectable.

In a nation like ours, long dedicated to the proposition that the artistic and the mundane should be kept apart, somewhat like church and state, a major *rapprochement* of the two—if that is what we are confronting—could on the face of it be suspicious. If the consumer is in fact abdicating his God-given right to say what he doesn't like about the latest in art, while the artist in turn, fattened by Ford Foundation subsidies, Federally sponsored exhibitions overseas, and dealer's high prices, has decided to make his work more or less innocuous, what have we here? It smacks of collusion.

Yet is the situation quite as grave as that? Abstract "action" painting, to be sure, is now at home on Main Street, and doubts have been raised about the soundness—the public-relations soundness, that is—of any major bank that doesn't own at least one Pollock or Kline. Yet lo! Now that "action" painting is a smashing success even in

Arkansas, what are many younger painters doing? Moving on from this proven formula to very different, bold experiments of their own, as the portfolio opening on page 17 indicates.

Has our contemporary ear become so generally attuned to atonality and the twelve-tone scale that Leonard Bernstein could safely play a work of this sort by Aaron Copland for the television masses at the show-off opening night of Lincoln Center without incurring sponsor trouble? Along comes a Lukas Foss (page 76), out to upset the established twelve-tone applecart with radical improvisations that batter the senses—hard.

Are we all growing accustomed—even inured—to the organized innovations and oddities of off-Broadway theatre? Along come such far-off-Broadway loners as the Coreys (page 88) with further innovations of a most personal sort, or the wholly unreconstructed rebels of London's Royal Court Theatre (page 26), evidently out to beat all comers about the head.

Whether all that these various nonconformists have to say in word, act, sound, or paint will make a winning impression on the generality, only time will tell. But though the New Frontier is thought to have established in America a climate more favorable to the arts than heretofore, there remains at the same time a new frontier in the arts themselves—and it may restore Murray Kempton's faith in them when he sees here that some things being done by far-out artists, writers, and musicians are still challenging and difficult to take.   W.H.H.

THEATRE

The Case for Repertory

The Metropolitan Opera is perhaps less venturesome than it need be, the New York Philharmonic is said to be suffering from excessive personal showmanship, the Museum of Modern Art has been accused of manipulating taste. Reforms are ever being urged on these and similar establishments, both in this country and abroad. But there is no dissenter so passionate that he would urge their abolition. The public knows instinctively that such institutions preserve the heritage of the arts they embody and provide standards to be met, excelled, or on occasion, rebelled against.

In Europe the dramatic theatre also maintains, and is sustained by, institutions—the Comédie Française, the Moscow Art Theatre, the Abbey Theatre, the national and regional companies of almost every European country. At the apex of the American theatre there is Broadway.

Broadway is not an institution, it is a phoenix. It dies on Memorial Day every year and is born anew on Labor Day. That may sound romantic and admirably indomitable, but in fact our theatre lacks the energy for this annual rebirth. Year by year, it becomes harder to break out of the egg, and Broadway grows more anxious, more opportunistic, more expensive. It cannot build a following because it provides no entity to which loyalty can be pledged. As a result, the New York theatre has no audience in a meaningful sense; it survives on consumers for whom it packages hits.

Where this leads can be seen in the forecast published by the New York *Times* last fall: "With a new season getting under way next month Broadway is talking about musicals and money. The musical picture is clear. The money situation is cloudy. The trend toward musical theatre grows. . . . Recent Wall Street activities have not been ignored by theatrical investors. Producers are finding it more difficult to raise money." The kind of money here in question is venture capital; it is available—when it is available—for the enrichment of its owners, not for the enrichment of the theatre. Art and cultural philanthropy do not come into the picture. Venture capital wants quick and handsome returns, and the best chance for that lies in the closest feasible replica of *The Music Man.*

It is thus against the background of Broadway's steady debasement that one should heed the current revival of interest in that perennial word of theatre hope: Repertory. Minneapolis is building for Sir Tyrone Guthrie the Guthrie Repertory Theatre; it will open this spring. For the past three seasons U.C.L.A. has had its own Theatre Group, run by John Houseman. Last fall the University of Michigan engaged a repertory group, the Association of Producing Artists, as "company in residence." Also in the fall the Ford Foundation announced grants totaling $6,100,000 to nine repertory theatres now operating in various parts of the country. In 1961–62 the National Repertory Theatre, its cast headed by Eva Le Gallienne, Faye Emerson, Scott Forbes, and Frederic Worlock, toured fifty cities and eight college campuses and played to a total audience of more than 250,000. It is seeking funds to augment its repertory—an ambition that earned it a pat on the back in the *Congressional Record* but no public funds. There are now, according to a recent *Life* survey, an astounding five thousand regional theatre groups in this country; a great many of them operate on a repertory basis.

For better or worse, however, the nerve center of American theatre is still New York, and one awaits with greatest anticipation the completion of the Vivian Beaumont Theater—described, in the words of its principal donor, as a house "designed with primary emphasis on the needs of a company presenting repertory"—now in construction under the great culture umbrella of Lincoln Center. The anticipation is somewhat chilled by anxiety, for the theatre will be in the hands of Robert Whitehead and Elia Kazan, two of the most spectacularly successful operators of the Broadway gamble.

Kazan's preliminary announcements have raised fears and hackles. The director has talked, for example, of making the classics vital in contemporary terms and avoiding the smell of the library; this sounds depressingly defensive. He hopes each year to offer two new plays by leading American playwrights, which would be snatching the bread right out of Broadway's mouth. He advocates the dramatization of novels, an idea that smells, not of the library, but of Hollywood, and is preposterous when set against the list of immortal plays that have not been seen in New York within living memory. He would use stars, would test his productions out of town, and promises a box-office scale not so much below the Broadway norm as to be awkwardly competitive. Since Broadway has priced itself out of the reach of its natural audience, this last resolve is particularly dismaying. However, Kazan is being given ample time for second thoughts.

It is not as though repertory were an unknown experiment. What it can do and the problems it presents (some of them peculiarly American problems) are known from many admirable and a few noble ventures. In the first place, however, what exactly is repertory? It is not stock, though both normally work with a resident company in a permanent house. Stock is the system whereby three, four,

or five plays are offered in successive runs of a week or more each. Joseph Papp's New York Shakespeare Festival is a season of stock. Repertory offers several productions simultaneously, playing a different work at each performance and varying the fare from week to week as new productions are added and as the public makes known its relative interest in the offerings. The Metropolitan Opera and the New York City Ballet are repertory companies. At present the only dramatic repertory in New York is the off-Broadway Living Theatre. It is a doctrinaire group and very uneven; it also shows a vitality and a purity of intention found nowhere else in town.

Stock is in many ways the easier system. The proprietors can concentrate on one play at a time. By hiring one or two actors specifically for each production, they can get along with a relatively small permanent cast. The storage of sets and costumes is not formidable, since only one physical production need be in the house. Finally, the public knows what is being offered in a given segment of the season. The one drawback—the great hazard—is that if a play does not succeed, the company is stuck with it for the duration of its run. And, unlike the situation on Broadway, a hit cannot turn into a bonanza because previous commitments limit its run. Stock theatre is necessarily cautious theatre—*Charley's Aunt* always seems a good idea.

Repertory requires a larger and more versatile company; it involves a constant handling of sets, costumes, and props, and considerable space for storing them; it demands an audience sufficiently interested to keep abreast of the program (the Met and Balanchine's ballet seem not to suffer much on this score). At the same time, repertory offers an organic season—steadily growing, continually responsive to public interest—that is unmatched for excitement and usefulness in any other form of theatre. It is the only system by which a play that makes a strong appeal to a limited audience can be allowed to reach that audience. Provided that the manager has some knowledge of and respect for the stage, there need never be a failure in repertory. A play that is shown only once in ten days can be as successful (and, in the end, can be shown as many times) as one that plays three performances out of seven—each fills its house. Eva Le Gallienne, who from 1926 to 1933 ran the Civic Repertory Company and gave New York the most consistently splendid theatre it has ever known, reports that in the first two seasons her house drew 45 per cent of capacity, in the third season it drew 75 per cent, and in the last two seasons, 95 per cent.

From time to time an editor made ingenious by laziness will concoct a feature story by asking a group of theatre notables for lists of an ideal repertory. These can be entertaining for the light they throw on the contributors. *Theatre Arts* compiled such a symposium for an anniversary issue back in 1941. Eugene O'Neill produced a list that looked like the curriculum for a postgraduate course in the tragic drama; Laurence Olivier submitted one that seemed to promise attractive roles for all his friends. Thornton Wilder fired back a furious paragraph in which he denounced American directors for their inability to handle great plays of the past without "veiled condescension." William Saroyan, unable to find just what he wanted in the accumulated wealth of centuries, asked that plays be composed for the mythical occasion from *Leaves of Grass; Tom Sawyer* and *Huckleberry Finn;* Chicago's intellectual life of the period 1905–1925; the slapstick comedies of Sennett, Roach, Langdon, and Co.; newsreels; and sports (particularly baseball, football, and track). At that, his instinct may have been right, for all such lists are basically frivolous: they assume something called the ten—or twelve or twenty—greatest, most appropriate, or most successful plays, whereas the essence of repertory is not a list but a process.

*R*epertory is not intended to supplant stock; certainly it is not meant to supplant the long-run commercial production. What it is intended to do is give the theatre the continuity, the depth of history, and the standards of invention and performance that every other public art derives from its institutions. What this means in a specific case can be impressive: from 1921 to 1929 the Cleveland Playhouse under the direction of Frederic McConnell offered its audience eighty-nine productions, including such diverse works of genius or enduring talent as *The Importance of Being Earnest,* thirteen plays by Shaw and five by Shakespeare, *The Great God Brown, The Wild Duck, Six Characters in Search of an Author, The Playboy of The Western World, R.U.R., Turandot, The School for Scandal,* the *Hippolytus,* and *He Who Gets Slapped,* to say nothing of such lighter fare as *The Truth About Blayds, The New York Idea,* and *Rollo's Wild Oat.* I do not know what the quality of these productions was, but the very list inclines me to believe it was high. When you are told that a diver has executed a full gainer with a half twist, you do not ask whether he did it well: there is no other way to do it.

Let us skip, as obvious, the joy of living within reach of such a cornucopia of theatre wealth, and consider it from a more specialized professional viewpoint. What would one think of a young writer who set out to be a novelist without having read, to pick at random, *War and Peace, Vanity Fair, Père Goriot,* and *Moby Dick*? Yet how many who launch themselves as playwrights have seen *Coriolanus,* the *Eumenides, The Seagull,* or *Peer Gynt*? They will have read them, perhaps, but in the case of plays, reading is a pale approximation of the live creation. It is like encountering masterworks of painting in reproduction.

One of the difficulties confronting an American repertory company, one of the reasons why it is harder to found and maintain one here than in Europe, is that America has no national heritage of drama to provide a proud base of operations. Consider what lies to the hand of a French, English, Russian, or Irish producer who may want to appeal to the patriotism of his audience, and compare these legacies with what the American producer can draw upon. When the point comes up here, everyone instantly mentions O'Neill and then babel ensues. Thornton Wilder, Maxwell Anderson, Lillian Hellman, Elmer Rice, Robert Sherwood, Arthur Miller, Tennessee Williams? Yes, all these and others who come perhaps less quickly to mind are suitable. Indeed, a function of repertory should be to keep the more enduring work of such craftsmen alive. Nonetheless, the planners are haunted by a suspicion that these names hardly qualify for Olympus: Where is the Shakespeare, the Molière, the Chekhov, the Ibsen? An all-American repertory would be composed entirely of excellent side dishes and no main course. With the possible exception of O'Neill, we have produced no dramatists of absolute rank—none to stand with the European immortals; none, for that matter, to stand with our own novelists: Melville, James, Hawthorne, Cooper, Twain, Dreiser, Hemingway, Faulkner.

Is that, perhaps, because we have provided no institutional theatre? It is a chicken-or-egg question, but at least it may be noted that Shakespeare had the Globe, Chekhov had the Moscow Art, Synge had the Abbey, and O'Neill himself had the Provincetown. It is probably safe enough to say that until we provide a great repertory house, endowed for and dedicated to excellence, a house in which playwrights can learn the language, history, and magic of their art, we shall produce no drama of the stature that gives a nation its place with other nations. We have a great deal of talent, but I am not speaking of that. Genius is another thing, and if O'Neill is a genius, as I think time may show he is, he is to date our only one.

Repertory in America, therefore, must acknowledge its native poverty and offer itself as a world stage. It must hope to develop a style that is at once receptive to a wide variety of sources and yet has a cohesive American texture. This in itself will require a kind of genius: Joseph Papp's seasons in Central Park and the New York City Ballet suggest that it is possible. The productions of these companies could have been created only in the United States. There is about them a lucidity, a colloquialism, a lean energy and youthful expression of delighted discovery that are essentially American. At the same time, they serve well their great European sources.

Lacking an obvious backlog of plays, the native repertory producer also lacks an obvious backlog of players. And here there is no question of the chicken or the egg. Our actors are not educated through apprenticeship; they are tuned up by competition in a commercial atmosphere where getting across is the goal. American actors learn to project themselves on an audience before they learn to propel themselves through a door. They become personal-

ities before they become professionals—if, indeed, they ever become that. I generalize unfairly, I know, for there are many fine actors on the American stage (though the best-trained, it seems to me, are usually in support of the glorious stars). But as a generalization the charge is accurate: our actors, deprived of the training of many seasons of steady and varied work, become set in narrow frames that exploit their natural gifts and do not expose their ignorance and inexperience. Guthrie once said that it is profitless to discuss an actor's ability until he has played a great classic role. How many of ours ever get the chance? Our star system, rigid and self-aggrandizing, is at the opposite pole from the virtues of repertory.

I would, however, expect the problem of actors to solve itself relatively quickly. As a class, actors show themselves eager students: you have only to note the alacrity with which young players desert opportunities on Broadway and in the studios to play in off-Broadway cupboards that offer instruction in the trade. By quickly, however, I do not mean instantly. Kazan, or anyone else who wants to assemble a group of players as accomplished, flexible, and harmoniously attuned to one another as the musicians in any first-class orchestra, will have to count on slow progress through a good many seasons. A director who lacks the patience or nerve for such a course, who wants or needs early applause, will shop for stars and shape his repertory to the names for hire. The result will be something like the American Shakespeare Festival at Stratford, Connecticut—opulent mediocrity.

*P*atience not only implies nerve, it implies money—a subject I have left to the last because I know little about it. Writing for *Theatre Arts* back in 1958, Oliver M. Sayler, a man who learned his trade with the Moscow Art Theatre and Max Reinhardt, warned that no one should attempt a full-scale repertory in an urban center until he had $3 to $5 million *for the company alone* safely stored in blue chip investments. Ongoing subsidy he rejected as much too chancy—it is the nature of angels that they lose their fervor after a time or suffer a clipping of their wings. Miss Le Gallienne, writing a few months later in the same magazine, endorsed Sayler's views from personal experience. The Civic Repertory died in 1933 because its private Croesus was not exempt from the Depression that then gripped the whole country.

Another warning from old repertory hands is that the management must never succumb to the temptation of sending a hit to Broadway for a straight run. It may look like quick and easy money, but the effect is to deprive the rest of the repertory of the support it must have. The company back in the home theatre collapses while the prodigal riots among the fleshpots.

The kind of money we are talking about now is not venture capital, but benevolent capital. It troubles some people that a theatre of high resolve should need to be endowed, but that is only because they have been conditioned by the finances of show business, where the only resolve is to make a killing. All orchestras are endowed, as are all opera and ballet companies, museums, libraries, colleges, and hospitals. So, in their own ways, are the U. S. Postal Service and the New York Rapid Transit System. Any facility set up for the benefit of society at large must depend on resources beyond its immediate income.

Lincoln Center is budgeted at present at $132 to $140 million for construction and land, $10 million for "education and artistic achievement." That works out at a ratio of fourteen to one for body and soul. I hope the soul is not being shortchanged. Particularly, I hope that Messrs. Whitehead and Kazan get a sum close enough to $5 million that they are not constrained to the jackdaw practices of Broadway. The Met and the Philharmonic come to Lincoln Center with an old tradition to sustain them; the repertory theatre must create a new image among all that new marble and plaster. Right now, the Vivian Beaumont Theater is the best chance for the revival of noble repertory in New York. But I should not like to think that it is the last or only chance.   ROBERT HATCH

BOOKS

Dreamer of Light and Dark

Carl Gustav Jung, one of the pioneers of modern psychology, was born in 1875, about twenty years after Freud, and died in 1961. He was the son of a poor Protestant clergyman in the German-speaking region of Switzerland. Glum, sensitive, introverted, he built his own fantasy-life during his school days, nearly died of loneliness and fear and accidie, and then compelled himself to recover and live vigorously. A scholarship took him to the University of Basel. He determined to emulate both his father, a parson, and his grandfather, a physician. After graduating in medicine, he became a spiritual healer. Throughout his life his main concerns were healing and preaching.

Healers and preachers must know much about their patients, they need reveal little about themselves. Neither Freud nor Jung wrote a full-length autobiography: their lives held too many secrets, some hidden even from themselves. However, seven years ago, that brilliant entrepreneur of the intellect, Kurt Wolff (the founder of Pantheon Books), suggested that a biography of Jung should be started while he was still alive. He was over eighty, but he was still active enough to help its maker. If too old to write a continuous narrative, he could answer questions and dictate paragraphs. His interrogator, Aniela Jaffé, managed to build a book out of her questions and his responses. Recently issued abroad in the original German, it is to appear here in the spring as *Memories, Dreams, Reflections,* in a translation by Richard and Clara Winston, published, naturally, by Pantheon.

Jung loved mythical patterns. He believed that, when properly understood, they could be used to make life easier and more fruitful. In his personal life he had played a number of mythical roles; and now, at its end, he became with his biographer the archetype of the Old Sage who is accompanied by a Young Woman as his attendant and interpreter. Her interrogation did not exhaust but stimulated him. After eighty years of determined reticence, he wrote down his own recollections of childhood and youth, which are the essential opening chapters of every biography; he added new material to other sections put together by Aniela Jaffé; and he composed a final meditation on the crisis that is tormenting the soul of the world.

The result is a peculiar and captivating work. Jung had a massively strong character, which communicated itself through everything he wrote. One of my strangest memories is of a week spent on jury duty some years ago. I was often called, and immediately dismissed when the lawyers learned I was a university professor, so I had plenty of time to read. Most of that week I spent reading a multivolume transcript of a seminar Jung gave in the thirties but would never permit anyone to publish. When my duty was over, my ears were full of the sound of his voice, with its dry witticisms and cool contempt for nonsense; and, at a distance of six thousand miles and twenty years, I had become one of his pupils. This powerful personality displaying itself in many unusual ways is one of the chief values of *Memories, Dreams, Reflections.*

In content it is unlike any other biography. Its main concern is not facts but dreams. Or rather—since dreams themselves are facts—it tells more of Jung's inner life than of his external career, and more of his visionary than of his intellectual adventures. Thus, we are given some data about his childhood and schooling but relatively little about his training as a doctor, his career after graduation, and his increasing success as a psychiatrist; much about his struggles to solve the problems presented to him by Christian religious doctrine, nothing whatever about his first awareness and experience of sex. His marriage, his wife, his children, are mentioned only in passing. What he dwells upon with the greatest zest and intensity are his dreams, or at least those which he could remember and interpret. Some are beautiful and significant for others.

Once, when visiting the United States with Freud, Jung dreamed he was exploring a house that was unknown to

him, although he felt he owned it. The upper story was relatively modern, but on going downstairs he found himself in a medieval room. Below that again was a vaulted cellar with Roman brickwork, and lower still, concealed beneath the foundations, a cave cut in the rock, containing bones, primitive pottery, and two ancient broken skulls. When he related this dream, Freud concentrated, not upon its structure and its mythical content—the descent into the depths and the discovery of more and more ancient dwellings beneath today's home—but upon the two skulls. Again and again he tried to get Jung to admit that he harbored death-wishes toward two people. At last—here is a curious fact—Jung said "My wife and my sister-in-law," knowing this to be false, but lying to preserve his relationship with the master. Jung then gives his own interpretation of the dream: the house was his psyche, which he was then and thereafter exploring, to discover, deeper and deeper within it, the remains of pre-Christian and then of prehistoric life.

It is odd that Jung himself should give a predominantly Freudian analysis of another of his important dreams, one which preoccupied him all his life. When he was between three and four, he dreamed of visiting an underground room like a palace, with a red carpet, a dais, and a golden throne. Upon the throne stood a being twelve or fifteen feet high, made of flesh and skin but limbless. It ended in a faceless, hairless head, and on the very top of this was a single eye. The child looked at it terrified, heard his mother's voice crying, "That is the man-eater!" and awoke sweating and trembling with fear. The being, says Jung, was a phallus, indeed a ritual phallus, which should mean that as a child he felt the danger and power of sex and symbolized it in this form. Yet he adds that he did not then know it as a phallus; and it is surely improbable that, at such an age and with such an upbringing, he could have seen and remembered the real object.

The context in which he narrates the dream is exclusively religious: his fear of Jesus and of Jesuits, his dread of deaths and interments. It appears to me that he *later* interpreted the being as a phallus because he was devoted to the idea that primitive archetypes are present even in the psyche of a little boy; and that we might more reasonably call it a childish attempt to visualize God—enthroned because king, limbless and huge because not human but superhuman, fleshly because alive, and—most important to small children brought up in a strict household—all-seeing. Look at the Great Seal of the United States on the back of any dollar bill, and you will see (adapted to conceptions that I believe to be Masonic) the same symbol. Jung even reports that the eye in his dream had a bright halo around it.*

His dreams persisted throughout his long life, not only when he was asleep. If I had a colleague who deliberately engaged in so many apparently irrational or inexplicable activities as did Jung, I should begin to worry about his teaching load. Approaching forty, he filled six notebooks

*To explain that, he gives an insecure etymology for "phallus," deriving it from an excessively rare Greek word meaning "white."

with his fantastic visions, and then rewrote them in calligraphic script in a folio volume embellished with his own drawings of the mandala—the complex pattern bounded by a circle, which means, and helps to make, psychical unity. Quite casually he observes that he had, at intervals, been visited by apparitions of grotesque and sinister faces. The house he built at Bollingen he kept changing, to represent changes in his own emotional life. From boyhood he carved mysterious symbolic figures in wood and stone. We think of Jung as a doctor, a healer. He thought of himself as a seer and a poet who was also a doctor: an artist, patterning subconsciously generated material in order to help his associated self, the scientist who used it practically.

In the end, the poet and artist became dominant: the scientist turned into the mystic. When he interpreted the work of the alchemists as being, not attempts to solve the problem of transmutation of metals, but rather symbolic exercises for healing and strengthening the psyche, many followed him with interest, but some turned away. When he began to write about astrology as though it were a solid body of truths, he lost disciples. Thus, in this very book, he says that "the appearance of Christ coincided with the start of a new aeon, that of the age of the Fishes. A synchronicity exists between the life of Christ and the objective astronomical event, the entry of the spring equinox into the sign of Pisces. Christ is therefore the 'Fish' . . . and emerges as the ruler of the new aeon." Interesting as poetry; as mystical endeavor to understand the interplay of human and superhuman, touching; but as science or history, sad. This is the kind of mysticism which occupied Yeats through much of his later life, which he set down in *A Vision,* and which issued in some of his finest poems; but Yeats was never regarded as a scientist, or even as a sage.

*T*here is much in Jung's work that I fail to understand. I cannot make out whether this is because it is often expressed in a special vocabulary, or because I have not read all his books, or because I lack the penetration, or because he sometimes talks nonsense, or because on certain subjects he is deliberately or unconsciously evasive. On one of the great permanent problems, the existence and nature of the deity, I think he usually speaks in riddles. Apparently he was convinced that there is only one God, although he does not say why. Perhaps he thought *one world = one divinity.* Yet often he seems to imply that God is a product, a projection, of the human psyche; and in a significant paragraph of *Memories, Dreams, Reflections,* he writes: "Through his consciousness man takes possession of nature by recognizing the existence of the world and thus, as it were, confirming the existence of the Creator. . . . If the Creator were conscious of Himself, He would not be in need of conscious creatures." And, for some reason which is hard to discover, Jung believed that all the different souls and minds of all the different races of mankind with all their different cultures and world views were basically one.

As the explorer of the human mind, Jung was convinced that it contained the central meaning of the universe. He was, it seems, unwilling to contemplate the vast metagalactic activity in time and space of which consciousness, human or other, is but one aspect, and which anyone who would apprehend godhead must regard as a totality. He looked inward, not outward. This does not mean that he contributed nothing to the problem of God. One of his strongest beliefs was that it is impossible to reconcile goodness with power. "I always fight against it," he said, "when the theologians say God is good. Master Eckhart says that God is not good, because if he were he would be better. This is true; and I would add that he loses his freedom because he is bound to be good, he can do nothing but good, which would be a great drawback to his omnipotence." In the final chapter of *Memories, Dreams, Reflections* Jung elaborates this, but at the same time beclouds it, by writing: "The myth must ultimately take monotheism seriously and set aside its dualism, which . . . has up to this time enthroned an eternal dark antagonist [Satan] beside the omnipotent Good."

Jung had a contemporary living near him, the Swiss poet Carl Spitteler (winner of the Nobel Prize in 1919) who, in a magnificent epic poem called *Olympian Spring*, grappled with the same problem. For Spitteler it was the strange character of the external cosmos, which seems to be hostile to life. For Jung it was the mystery of the psyche: the arcanum crudely stated in the doctrine of "original" sin inherited from father Adam, that all human beings are both evil and good at heart, and that each of us must learn to harmonize his dissonant soul, to create a universe which he can, without destroying himself or others, for a little time inhabit.   GILBERT HIGHET

MOVIES

The Mass-produced Insight

American films were slow to catch up with psychology. Quite early, the Germans caught the modern psychological fever. *The Cabinet of Dr. Caligari* (1919), a strange and powerful picture on the theme of mental aberration, brought together the expressionist innovations of Strindberg and the atmosphere of Central European psychiatry. But the American movie makers of the twenties did not care for that sort of thing. They were curiously, even obstinately, old fashioned. It is odd to think that Freud's *Interpretation of Dreams* (1900) and the nickelodeon are approximately contemporary. And in the twenties, while Mary Pickford and Lillian Gish were thriving on the screen, so were Jung and Ferenczi in psychology, James Joyce in literature, Klee and Picasso in painting. Evidently the movie makers of that not-so-remote time were dragging their feet. Perhaps they correctly interpreted the desire of the public not to be hurried at the same rate of speed along every level of development.

Whatever the reasons, Hollywood continued for a long time to make action films. Cowboys, Indians, pioneers, cops and robbers, doughboys and Krauts, rags and riches, gave it all the material it needed. But slowly the movies became psychological. Plain goodness, blunt badness, the honor of strong silent men, simple love, and classical jealousy went out of fashion. Hollywood went on making action pictures, of course, but significant actions became harder to find as we entered this present age of upheaval and disarray. We could no longer take the old virtues straight. It was necessary to be reconciled to them indirectly, and for this purpose Hollywood created a popularized Freudianism. A new kind of "insight," used at first as an ornament or gimmick, presently became the main reliance of the movie script-writer.

For richer or for poorer, as the marriage service goes, in health but especially in sickness, we are now wedded to this new movie psychology. About ten years ago a shrewd and gifted movie critic, Manny Farber, noted the change in an article called "Movies Aren't Movies Any More" and subtitled "The Art of the Gimp Takes Over." The Gimp was a mechanical device used by Victorian lady golfers. It lifted their skirts for one flashing instant to enable them to hit the ball. "Something like this device has now been developed in Hollywood," wrote Farber. "Whenever the modern film maker feels that his movie has taken too conventional a direction and is neglecting 'art,' he need only jerk the Gimp string, and behold—curious and exotic but psychic images are flashed before the audience, pepping things up at the crucial moment, making you think such thoughts as 'The hero has a mother complex,' or 'He slapped that girl out of ambivalent rage at his father-image which he says he carries around in his stomach.'"

Since Farber wrote his article, the psychological revolution has been completed. The public has been thoroughly trained. It can be depended upon to take up every cue given by the film maker. "Insight," a proud word for things that millions of people have learned by rote, stands now in the very center of the entertainment industry. Often the plot and all the actions of a movie are derived from a nucleus of psychological illumination. Heroes are those who struggle heroically with neuroses, while villains are afflicted with sadistic or sadomasochistic difficulties that we are invited to understand sympathetically, with Hollywood insight. Even the action film—the western, the spectacular, the thriller—is now constructed on this principle.

Ten years ago a movie like Alfred Hitchcock's *Psycho* would have been simply *The Mad Murderer*—tried and true Grand Guignol. The old tricks still work: the blood of the murdered woman swirls in the drain of the shower stall, the slaughtered detective struck by his unseen assailant falls backward down a flight of stairs. The effects are so broad that we smile as we shudder. We have come to be kidded by a master, and he does not let us down. But how different things are now! Our murderer is the victim of an unhealthy Oedipal love. He keeps his mummified mother in the coal cellar and commits his crimes dressed in her clothes. When the mystery is solved and the criminal apprehended, the action moves to a mental hospital. A psychiatrist invites us to view the murderer as a clinical subject; there are no more punishments, only explanations.

So we sit patiently as the psychiatrist lectures us. His confident, rather ignorant and platitudinous words conclude the picture. The poor transvestite murderer is left looking quietly psycho in his mother's very unstylish clothes. In a cruder day, he would have fallen from the roof or failed to beat a train to the crossing. *Nous avons changé tout cela.* Young Perkins is even shown to us as a wholesome, winsome, sincere-looking American youth—a type that Hollywood has taught us to mistrust. There *are* no handsome, winsome Johnnies any more: their corruption has been exposed to our insight.

It is utopian to expect Hollywood movies without this sort of thing. In *Spartacus* the Roman jailers are voyeurs. In *Butterfield 8* the distress of Elizabeth Taylor is caused by a wicked old friend of the family who corrupted her when she was a little child. In *The Hustler* the young lovers are clearly stamped, face and form, with the psychological Hollywood look. Brave soldiers of fear, they seek, in skill with a pool cue, in drink and in love, to free themselves from neurosis. But there is an evildoer who perversely envies the pair and destroys them with psychological poisons. In *The Misfits* each portion of the action is followed instantly by an appropriate insight. On one side are ranged, thematically, insights into beauty and love, happiness, instinct, liberty, and creativity, and on the other side stand the opposing vices—misery, hate, the impoverished imagination, money, and death. A movie so intensely instructive in purpose might more effectively have been presented as an old-fashioned morality play, with each abstraction clearly labeled. As it is, the realism of *The Misfits* simply gets in the way. We have to wait nearly an hour, watching a laborious accumulation of evidence, to discover that the young divorcee (the late Marilyn Monroe) represents It— the Life Force itself.

The difficulty is that movie problems, movie insights, have come to be more interesting by far than the characters whom they preoccupy or afflict. The actors in a movie occasionally remind us of the models in a fashion magazine. The models have no human qualities: they merely wear the merchandise. Consider a recent picture like *Summer and Smoke,* adapted from the play by Tennessee Williams. Its characters can never really convince us that they are human beings; they are animated postulates, figures in a plight—they are showing off the goods. The heroine is a repressed Southern girl. Her glaucous eyes, in brilliant color, reveal all in a single glance. Her Mama is a kleptomaniac, much attached to the bottle. She, too, is a familiar figure. She has been going strong ever since *The Little Foxes,* when she was known as Aunt Birdie. But now we have more insight into the type. We understand how it is with people who tipple and steal hats from the milliner: anyone who steals compulsively suffered a deprivation of love during the crucial years of development.

The hero, too, is a psychological type. He is mixed up with some wild, Dionysiac, bayou folk, rather drearily put together from the leftovers of an old Mexican picture. The young doctor's brilliant red roadster is a welcome sight, a far more dynamic object than any of the young ladies who are chasing Laurence Harvey, its driver. But we know that the car is something else, too. And so we wait, seasoned veterans of boredom that we are, for the real thing. That is revealed to us when the young doctor pulls down an anatomical chart and says to our heroine, whose gaze is desperately thickened by the drugs she has been swallowing to help her bear her unrequited love: "Do you know what this is? This is a man!" Or, in the dialect of the region, "a ma-un!"

It is now that we know we are about to transact the real business of the evening, and this business has nothing to do with the South, or with cars, or with alleged bayou people. It has to do mainly with the psychological issues. The occasion is one for "insight." It is didactic. We have come to learn something. Perhaps it would be more correct to say that we have come to rehearse a lesson, and this lesson is that Puritanical repression is an evil, that the instincts are not to be mocked, that the body is a sacred object, and that sex, properly understood, is a form of holy worship.

*S*uch beliefs, held in the past by radical artists and thinkers, are now offered daily to mass audiences by the large circulation magazines and the television industry and other molders of public opinion. The public is being taught new standards, and it is *that,* the liberalization of opinion, which has become the dramatic event in the movie house. This liberalization has developed its own form of piety. People feel about these popular insights that they are moral, and movie psychology thus turns out to be a popular sort of moralizing.

What André Malraux rather bitterly calls "the arts of delectation"—he classes the popular novel with the movies—are being used for Improvement (a Victorian term for Upgrading). Americans are in general sensitive to their responsibilities, and when they confront the great public, they feel a very particular responsibility to instruct it. And they have instructed it. But somehow the new excitement of Hollywood's psychological morality is not as great as the old excitement of the action film. This new excitement is the excitement of belonging to the vanguard of enlightenment, a triumphant private sense of being in the know, of the confirmation of judgments we believe to be our own. It gives us the illusion that we are thinking seriously about life.   SAUL BELLOW

CHANNELS

Suds in Your Eye

Before 1962 is entirely forgotten, like 1467 and 12 B.C., there appear to be a few loose ends that might as well be tied up. It wasn't the worst of years, as years have been going lately, and it deserves a decent burial.

The most remarkable statement of the year, as far as I can establish, was made late in the summer to a reporter for the New York *Times* by a gentleman named William P. Orr, who presides over the television activities of Warner Brothers in far-off Hollywood. Mr. Orr was unburdening himself, as tycoons will, of his deeper thoughts concerning the future of television, and in doing so seems to have remarked: "Dramas about peace, no matter how many criminals you use, can't be as exciting as a war." Before considering this apophthegm in all its fruitiness, we will have to give it a wash and polish job. Let us assume, to begin with, that Mr. Orr really intended to say that dramas about peace can't be as exciting as *dramas* about a war. At least, I hope that is what he means, because the head of television at Warner Brothers throws a lot of weight, and if he is suggesting we should all march off to war instead of watching the Du Pont Show of the Week, there is a slim chance he can bring it off. I am also going to assume that by "criminals" he doesn't really mean criminals, but kindly men from Central Casting pretending to be criminals.

Thus freshened up to meet company, his remark is certainly as provocative as anything I found in the *Times* all year. It casts an entirely new look on drama, television,

and Mr. Orr. I had never enjoyed so clear a vision where drama was concerned; it had never occurred to me, until Mr. Orr set me straight, that there would be criminals in dramas about peace, and if it had occurred to me, I would never have thought of counting them. Hereafter I shall expect all theatre critics dealing with dramas about peace to count the criminals and let me know.

It might also be worthwhile to quote another of Mr. Orr's gems, out of the same interview: "It would be difficult for anyone to object to violence in a war series. You can't have war without violence, so I don't think we can be accused of violence for violence's sake." This appears to be a neatly rounded thought, and will therefore pass without comment.

In the somewhat more private domain of my own immediate neighborhood, 1962 was made memorable by a young lady of my acquaintance who set up house for herself and soon afterward visited the supermarket. Among the products she carried home were fifteen different kinds of soap, all of which she assured me were absolutely essential if a lady was to keep a tidy pad.

I was dubious, but I am no expert on soap so I telephoned a chemist down the street and asked him how many kinds of soap there are. "One kind," he said promptly. "You wash things with it." I do not wish to suggest that the chemist's world and the housewife's world are quite the same thing, but nevertheless I have a grave suspicion that what my friend bought was one kind of soap and fifteen kinds of labels, not that I see what harm *that* does.

It made me realize, however, that soap manufacturers seem to be more at peace with each other than most rugged individualists. Each of them produces a whole battery of soaps, under different names, and then they all encourage the buyer to shop around, buying soap for one purpose from one maker, and soap for another purpose from another maker, until all of them have sold a little soap and the industry thrives. Other manufacturers take a much narrower view. There aren't any more different kinds of cigarette than there are different kinds of soap, but the cigarette manufacturers aren't nearly so live and let live; each of them insists you smoke his brand and no other. It would be far more genteel if there were one brand for rainy days, and one for hard-to-manage mouths, and one that you stocked up on simply because it floated.

As far as the advertising industry itself was concerned, 1962 was not a vintage year, by any means. What entertainment there was seemed to be limited to a private game being played in New York, Chicago, and Los Angeles, in the form of advertising that was directed, not at the general public, but at the advertisers themselves. This sort of thing is supported by magazines, for example, which take full-page advertisements in newspapers in the hope of cajoling advertisers into taking full-page advertisements in magazines. The preceding sentence may be somewhat hard to follow, but it is the best I can do and if you read it over a few times it will begin to make sense—or rather, to be coherent. I would rather not say whether I think it makes sense or not.

The oddity of this sort of thing is not evident until you realize that as soon as this advertising is placed, the men who have placed it go out and have lunch with the people they are advertising at. The world of advertising is not so extensive that it takes a full-page advertisement in the *Times* to establish communication; it's just one big family, most of which lives in a tenement named Madison Avenue. The big problem is keeping something a secret, not making it known.

Actually, this strange stentorian dialogue arises out of the nature of the ad man himself. Part of the pathology of advertising is that it creates in the ad man, who certainly ought to know better, an incredible credulity about anything he sees in print or hears as a commercial on television. This credulity is probably essential if he is to retain his sanity: if he begins scoffing at other men's copy, he may one day learn to scoff at his own. Thus, if he is merely told, over a table, at the "21" Club, that *McCall's* is selling so many copies a month that the Province of Quebec will soon be as bare of trees as Track 14, Lower Level, he simply looks sly, lets one eyelid droop knowingly, and generally lets it be known that he wasn't born yesterday. Tell him the same thing on the back page of his morning daily, however, and he takes it as gospel.

Metropolitan papers were kept solvent last year by this sort of thing. *McCall's* and the *Ladies' Home Journal* were screaming invective at each other every third morning,

reaching a grand climax when *McCall's* announced that it was cutting prices for color advertisements and the *Ladies' Home Journal* was so put out that it shouted foul and fell to the canvas clutching its profit-and-loss statement. *Good Housekeeping,* which had nothing in particular to say about the whole thing, kept taking full-page ads to say that it had nothing to say. Mind you, this had nothing whatsoever to do with those who actually buy the magazines, and may even read them. It was all infighting, carried on at premium rates.

*L*ocally, by which I mean New York, the event of the year was the return to the air waves of Bert and Harry Piel. To those who are remote from such matters, it may be necessary to explain that Bert and Harry Piel are two cartoon characters, created and given tongue by a comedy team called Bob and Ray, who shill for Piel's beer. They were the talk of the town when they were performing a few years back, largely because they were very funny. The only trouble was that everyone talked but few bought beer, and after a while Piel's dropped them, taking the view that they had stocked up on a lot of malt and hops and weren't in business just to amuse the television audience. The brewery has since changed hands, and the new owners are grimly determined to try again. They are very good commercials, and I listen to them whenever I can. I've never tried the beer.

So much for 1962. Now we have twelve fresh months ahead of us, in which almost anything can happen. Maybe Rosser Reeves will write another book. Surely William P. Orr has something more to say. I can hardly wait.

STEPHEN WHITE

Mr. Zeckendorf and Architecture: A Communication

To the Editor:

Caricatures may be a necessary part of American life, but the recent cartoon of William Zeckendorf published in the July issue of HORIZON under the title "A Modern Bestiary" I find impossible to classify as humor.

I have known Mr. Zeckendorf since the days when he had the courage and foresight to assemble the site on the East River which made it possible for the Rockefeller family to offer the United Nations a home in the center of our city.

Mr. Zeckendorf has been a constant supporter of good architectural design. For excellence in design, several of the projects which he has built since World War II have received national awards from such organizations as the American Institute of Architects.

His Kip's Bay housing project at 31st Street and First Avenue, designed by I. M. Pei, is one of the outstanding housing projects built any place in the world in the last ten years.

I know of no one who, as a private investor, has done more than Zeckendorf to eliminate slums and establish decent housing standards in this country.

Are these the reasons that led you to say "Naturalists believe it instinctively builds drab buildings the way the beaver builds leaky dams"?

By way of proof I enclose some pictures of his projects.

WALLACE K. HARRISON

Mr. Zeckendorf, a HORIZON subscriber, is indeed one of the country's most imaginative and active large-scale builders. We are sure he is able to recognize a caricature and the spirit of humor in which it was published. The vast array of Zeckendorf buildings, spanning a wide range of architectural accomplishment, does indeed include some outstanding examples of handsome architecture. The group below includes three of Reader Harrison's selections, and three others.—The Editors

© EZRA STOLLER

SKYVIEWS, N.Y.

Mile High Center, Denver   Denver Hilton and Department Store   Kip's Bay Plaza, New York City

112 West 34th Street, New York City   139 East 33rd Street, New York City   Park West Village, New York City

CLOUDS ON THE HORIZON

Who's Underdeveloped?

Almost all the world outside the Iron Curtain—even the new, liberal, constitutional, anti-colonialist, free, one-party African world—has been laughing for some years now at all those silly claims from Moscow that Russians invented everything. For now the secret is out at last: Africans did all that inventing, and if anyone doesn't believe it, here is official proof, put forward by Africans themselves.

The great moments in science and invention shown in the pictures below come from postcards recently received from Ghana in West Africa. They have a governmental air to them because they were made as reproductions of a set of murals called *Ancient African History,* by one Earl Sweeting, for the "Archive of Accra," the capital of the bustling, touchy, one-party state that Kwame Nkrumah, its combination Caesar and Kingfish, has forged out of the former British Gold Coast. Further investigation reveals that the "Archive of Accra" is actually the lobby wall of Nkrumah's Convention People's Party national headquarters building—as though our National Gallery hung its pictures in the smoking room of Tammany Hall.

Lest any purchaser of the postcards think that the boasts shown on them are idle ones, or that Africans did not in fact invent chemistry, architecture, the alphabet, short-hand, and the like, references—fine, scholarly references in the approved English textbook style—are included on the backs of the cards. Let us investigate those given on the reverse of the card (below left) in which Ham is shown teaching the alphabet to his brothers Shem and Japheth. (Never mind how Noah managed to have one thoroughly Negroid and two thoroughly Caucasian sons by the same wife; we are keeping Biblical controversy out of this.)

"*Ref*: Bernard Quaritch, *Palaeography,* 1894, p. 5; C. F. Volney, *The Ruins,* p. 17," runs the legend on the card. Quaritch, who was a London publisher and bibliophile, indeed ascribed an invention to Ham, although the invention, unfortunately, is that of writing, which is not quite the same thing as the alphabet. It also turns out that Quaritch used "Ham" in the normal figurative sense to mean the peoples of the Nile Valley; that is, the Hamitic branch of the Caucasian race and not the so-called Black Africans of the sub-Sahara region. In fact, calling Negroes

"Africans taught the Greeks the Alphabet. Ham teaching his Brothers Shem and Japheth the Alphabet." This is the legend on the back of this Ghana postcard. As full brothers, Noah's sons seem to show remarkable differences.

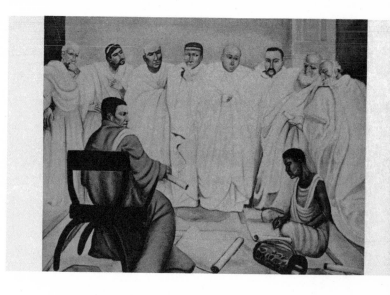

"Tyro, African Secretary to Cicero, originated short-hand writing in 63 B.C.*" Whether the slave-secretary was African, or a Negro as shown, history does not say, but it is probable that Cicero did his dictating more privately.*

the "sons of Ham" is rather an Old South idea, born in the era when plantation owners were hunting for religious justification for slavery and found something they thought would do in Genesis 9:22–27, where poor Ham is condemned to perpetual servitude. What the Hamites invented was hieroglyphics, not the Phoenician alphabet, and so, perhaps it would be wise to drop Quaritch altogether and try Volney—but what an embarrassment! Volney, an eighteenth-century writer, is here concerned with the rise and fall of empires and not Ham or the alphabet at all.

So much for that. In the case of shorthand (opposite right) one "ref." refers us to Conyers Middleton, *The Life of Marcus T. Cicero,* and there, sure enough, we find Tyro—generally spelled Tiro—as the great man's slave and secretary, although Middleton fails to mention any African background. Leaving these unco-operative refs. aside, various encyclopedias, including the *Britannica* (11th Edition), the *Italiana,* and the *Grand Larousse,* credit Tiro with inventing a system of shorthand but do not bring up his ancestry. Pauly's *Real-Encyclopädie* suggests that his name is of Palestinian or Persian origin, and Mitzschke, in *The Father of Stenography,* comes right out and says that Tiro was born in 103 B.C. at Arpinum, to a Roman slave. Could it be, in showing Tiro as a Negro, that somebody in Accra is stretching matters?

Turning now, with mounting concern, to chemistry, "originated by Africans in the ancient Empire of Ghana" (below left), we find four impressive references. One of them discusses early chemical knowledge in Egypt, but none of the books, unfortunately, backs up or even mentions the Ghana claim in any way. One of the four references, alas, is the long-deceased C. F. Volney, mentioned earlier when he was not writing about Ham. He was not writing about chemistry either, or even Africa. But who, after all, is going to cavil about little slip-ups like these? Documentation is the sleepy magic of the European. Who wants to waste the golden hours in a stuffy library in Accra when out in the golden sunshine a whale has beached and died and Kwame Nkrumah, the Osagyefo himself, is conducting a state funeral to placate the soul of the departed king of the sea? Maximum Leader, Maximum Fish, Maximum Research—is not Africa great, and Ghana greatest of all?

Commenting not long ago on Nkrumahism and its strange blend of polite forms, boastful manners, and primitive beliefs, one old African hand observed that "underdeveloped countries tend to have underdeveloped governments." After the recent bomb attack on Nkrumah, for instance, the official party newspaper, *The Evening News* of Accra, censured several officials, linking them to the unsuccessful plot in this wonderful mixture of voodoo, Biblical reference, and argument *ad hominem*:

On Friday, August 24, we editorially warned that evil hands of Kulungugu [the place of the bomb attack], whether they belonged to Philistines Essau or a new generation of Judases shall never endure. They shall be crushed. Today some of the villains have been unmasked in the persons of arch Judas Adamafio, lean and lanky Cassius Ako Adjei and ideologically bankrupt, potbellied Cofie-Crabbe.

In a land where one can dream, need anything lie between the wish and the consummation, between the fact and the fancy, between history and (if you will pardon the expression) invention?　　　　　OLIVER JENSEN

"The Science of Chemistry was originated by Africans in the ancient Empire of Ghana," says the caption, with respectful capitals. Chemistry, of course, did not "originate" anywhere all at once, but gradually, in many ancient lands.

"Architecture was originated by African mothers in laying foundations for building construction." Any neo-colonialist who doubts this statement is probably a paid Greek or Sumerian propagandist, not to mention an enemy of Mother Love.

DON'T CALL ME; I WON'T CALL YOU EITHER

The File on

an Article that Never Got Written

Recently a writer who has appeared frequently in HORIZON, the American John Keats, wrote to his literary agent, Sterling Lord, to propose another article for this magazine. Mr. Lord forwarded the letter to the editors, among whom it was circulated with these consequences:

Mr. Sterling Lord
The Sterling Lord Agency
75 East 55th Street
New York 22, New York

Dear Sterling:

    I am thinking again about Horizon, this time with regard to the telephone. I regard this instrument as the most uncalled-for disaster since the Flood. I feel a great sympathy for the Englishman who, answering the ring, inquires "Are you there?"--clearly indicating his doubt that anyone could really be there, and his morbid fear that someone might be.

    As you know, when Herr Reiss invented this contraption one luckless day in 1861, he named it (in his Greek) far-away sound. But, as you also well know, the sound of it is not far away. Indeed, its noise has become so omnipresent that it has turned America into a nation of telephone compulsives, jumping to the sound of bells like 180,000,000 Pavlovian mongrels. (Herr Reiss would be astounded; to him, the telephone was simply a little laboratory toy. But since he was a scientist, he can be excused on the grounds he did not know what he was doing. As Engine Charlie Wilson so succinctly said, "Basic research is when you don't know what you're doing.")

    At any rate, the story I have in mind would include the man perched on the New York hotel window ledge, fourteen stories above ground zero, trying to solve a personal problem. Two floors beneath him, the firemen were attempting to arrange a large net without attracting his attention. Above him, the cops were debating the best way of getting at him. To one side, from an adjoining window ledge, the priest they use on these occasions was reciting the stock exhortations. But across town, a nimble-witted reporter, understanding the American soul, simply put in a call to the hotel room. The phone rang; the wretch at once obeyed the conditioned reflex, quitting his ledge to answer it.

    Thus, too, when the Morro Castle was burning, a Chicago paper scooped the country simply by putting in a call to the ship. In the midst of holocaust, someone answered.

    The article would consider those who have tried--and failed--to work out an accommodation with the telephone; to construct defenses against it, or means to circumvent it. It would include anecdotes of telephone protocol, such as that of the two New York friends who wanted to lunch together, but whose jealous secretaries, insisting on their own prerogatives and defensive of their assumed differences in rank and the presumed importance of their bosses, kept the two men apart for more than a week. In the end, Bill quit trying to reach Joe on the phone. He simply walked across the street, into the elevator, got off at Joe's floor, barged into Joe's office, and said "Joe, how's about lunch?" Whereupon they went off to the Players.

    The article would also show what it means to live without a telephone--and how this is no defense. For instance, in summer my family and I live on an island without one, and find that we are invariably called to the mainland to answer the thing. We have to pay the boatman for bringing this message, and the message never comes except during hurricanes, or when the harmattan is blowing, and we have an open boat. Somebody Up There does not like us. En passant, the point would be made that when Bell Tel charges you more for an unlisted number, this is the same thing as a Chicago gangster offering you protection. (As the ultimate descendant of the only Saxon family to refuse to pay Danegeld, I will have none of this.)

    Among other points to be made are that the telephone is an unmitigated invasion of privacy, a time-waster, the source of morbid perforations of the gut, a damnable nuisance, and an endless opportunity for women to gabble. I find myself unable to regard with serenity those courses in telephony offered in the public schools. In some progressive dame schools, the children are sat at little desks with little dummy telephones, and learn to dial and answer; in high school, this education is carried on at a higher level: the kids are shown color movies that teach them how to make long-distance calls. The play phones, the instruction books, and the color films are provided by Bell.

    There are other things to say. At this point, however, I pass this on, in the hope that it strikes a responsive chord in the editorial minds of Messrs. Hale and Larrabee. The reason why I would like to place the piece with them is, when you write for Horizon, you do not have to presume the readers move their lips.

                        Sincerely,

                        John Keats

TO: William Hale

FROM: Eric Larrabee

I must say I think very well of Keats's proposal on the telephone. Some years ago I did a little blast on the same theme for Harper's Magazine, at the time when the Telephone Company was trying to get you to answer the phone by giving your name. They distributed blotters, for example, with thereon the legend: "Who is hello?" The increase in the charge for unlisted numbers came along some years later, and I believe it was the New York Post which pointed out that the logical extension of this would be to charge people even more for having no telephone at all.

People have tried to cope with the monster in a variety of ways. I have heard of brave souls who solve the problem of the loquacious caller by hanging up when they themselves are speaking, on the theory that no one could believe such a willful act of self-abnegation to have taken place. (Historically speaking, the bravest gesture of this kind is recorded by Quentin Reynolds, who claims to have been in President Roosevelt's office one day when someone hung up on F.D.R. The President was engaged in delivering a lecture on Far Eastern policy to Secretary Stimson, who rightfully felt that he had invented most of it and was, in addition, the only man in the Administration with a sufficient combination of character and pure gall.)

There is really something essentially nightmarish about the telephone, as the late James Thurber understood so well. Telephones figure often in his stories and cartoons, especially the one with the magnificent and unanswerable line: "If this is the wrong number, why did you answer the phone?" Someone described recently the thoroughly Thurberian disaster which occurred to a man who had two telephones on his desk. They seemed to have gone completely wacky; they would ring and ring, but each time he picked one up he would get nothing but a dial tone. What had happened, of course, was that he had put each receiver down on the cradle of the other.

Let us by all means encourage this charming proposal.

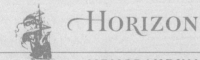

TO: William Hale

FROM: Ralph Backlund

By all means! But to encompass the full horror of the situation, Keats should not neglect the perils of recent developments such as all-number numbers (who can remember them?) and long-distance dialing--not to mention the bland assumption of the telephone company that the customer is always wrong. I know somebody in Connecticut who was charged on his bill for a call to San Francisco that he never made. When he protested that he not only had not made the call, but didn't know a soul in San Francisco, the business office agreed to look into the matter. A short time later they called back to say that he didn't need to know anyone in San Francisco, because the number called was the one they use out there to get the correct time.

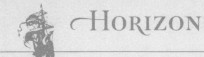

TO: William Hale

FROM: Albert Bermel

Yes, long-distance is the telephone company's ultimate weapon, mysterious, anonymous, remote; when it comes at you there is no way of striking back. An acquaintance reported recently that he was laboring through a tricky legal document when the phone tinkled. As he picked it up a voice said: "Long distance. May I help you?" He considered this, and replied, "I don't think so. May I help you?" There was a click and he found himself listening to the dial tone. Two minutes later the routine was repeated. It took him thirty minutes or so to get back into the spirit of the legal document.

There are other phone indignities I (and perhaps Mr. Keats) would like explained. Who, for example, called the multiple sclerosis people during one of their "telethons" and offered them $2,000 in my name? Who gave the neighborhood merchants my number the very day a new phone was installed so that they could spend that first evening competing for my dry-cleaning dollar? Couldn't the Bell research boys work up a modest machine that would levy an automatic charge on Encyclopedia Britannica salesmen, insurance operatives proposing "increased coverage," and Arthur Murray representatives who begin their spiel with, "You have just won first prize in an unofficial contest that entitles you to a free lesson at . . ."? These contributions, however small, would help to pay that basic monthly charge that gives a telephone subscriber the privilege of being at the world's mercy.

Mr. Sterling Lord
The Sterling Lord Agency
75 East 55th Street
New York, New York

Dear Mr. Lord:

I am going to make you and John Keats an odd proposal. His letter outlining an article about the menace of the telephone has drawn a flock of applauding memoranda here, each editor adding supporting instances from the wellsprings of comparable suffering. Looking over the dossier--for that is what it has now become--the thought occurred to me that it could be published as it stands, in lieu of John Keats's proceeding with the article itself. Are you and he game to this (subject to terms, of course)?

Cordially,

William Harlan Hale

Mr. William Harlan Hale
Editor, HORIZON
551 Fifth Avenue
New York, N. Y.

Dear Mr. Hale:

I see your point. I had wanted to tell, for instance about the last man in the Washington, D.C., directory, whose problems are as grotesque as they are frighteningly real; but we can skip it. (His problem--in the latest Washington directory in my hands, it was one H. A. Zvolovsky--is that Capital reporters have a way of telephoning the incumbent, just for the hell of it, to ask him what as last man his opinion is on atomic testing or Cuba or whatever; and I understand there are other jokers who also bedevil him with calls at any time of night simply to say, "So you're the last man in Washington's book.") Please feel free to call me (collect) at any time when we are again in such total agreement that writing the article has become superfluous.

Sincerely,

John

John Keats

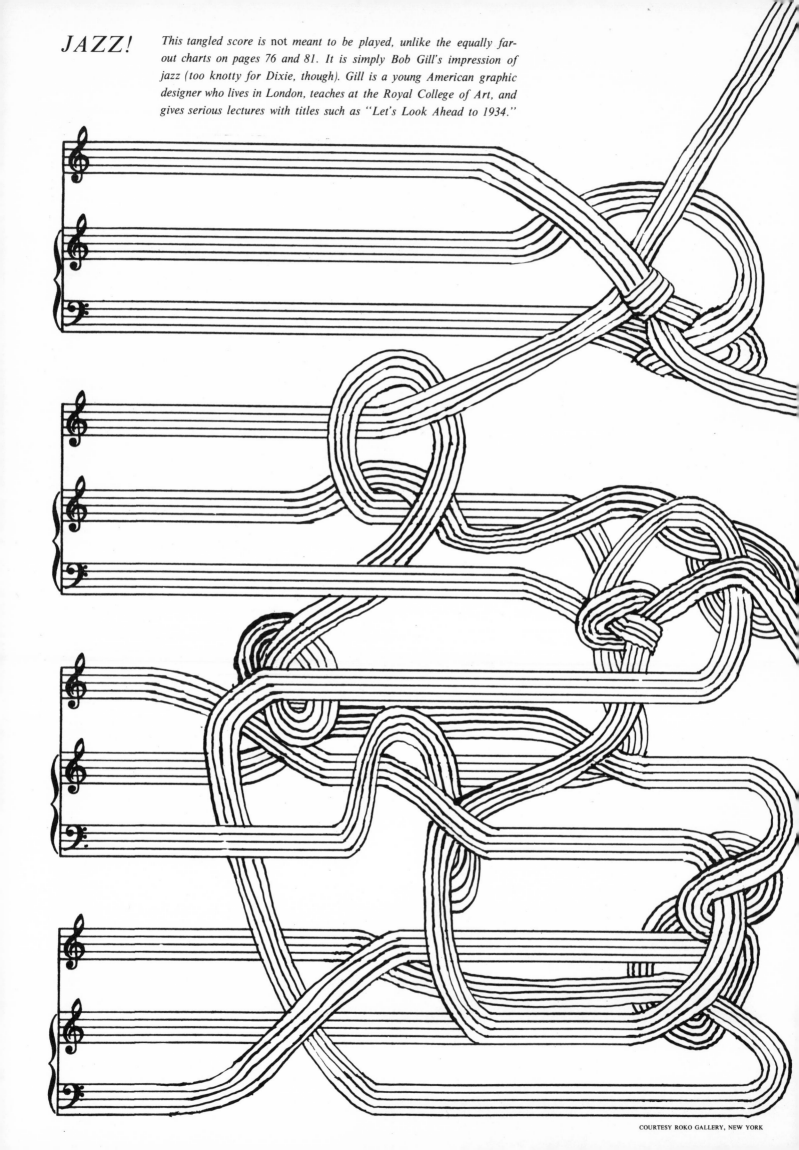

JAZZ!

This tangled score is not meant to be played, unlike the equally far-out charts on pages 76 and 81. It is simply Bob Gill's impression of jazz (too knotty for Dixie, though). Gill is a young American graphic designer who lives in London, teaches at the Royal College of Art, and gives serious lectures with titles such as "Let's Look Ahead to 1934."